Nelson
ENGLISH
DEVELOPMENT
BOOK 5

JOHN JACKMAN
WENDY WREN

Nelson

Contents

Writing	Personal Choice
observing and recording – descriptive research drafting and redrafting	pros and cons descriptive narrative research – fact file
characterisation drafting and redrafting	factual writing opinions narrative
narrative – ghost story descriptive drafting and redrafting	imaginative pros and cons personal experience
narrative – stories in other worlds conversation drafting and redrafting	book covers/blurb diary extract
persuasive language/layout visual appeal/comparison	opinion/factual/advertisement
imaginative – eye-witness account/reported account research – factual report	personal letter/interview research – graphic presentation
persuasive writing filling in form/business letters	travel poster/personal letter factual – graphic presentation
poetry and purpose similes and metaphors	descriptive personal opinion narrative
opinions – discursive writing drafting and redrafting	narrative poster discursive
summaries personal opinion discursive writing drafting and redrafting	imaginative advertisements personal
comparisons – analysis personal response fables	playscript fable
mystery story – narrative personal response	book cover/blurb imaginative – factual report
playscript personal response	narrative personal letter/poetry
prediction/narrative book reviews	book cover/blurb conversation
comparisons – purpose/style	purpose and audience – a choice of various writing styles: factual/personal narrative/descriptive

City life

'Market Scene, Northern Town, 1939' by L S Lowry, City of Salford Museums and Art Galleries

PICTURE STUDY

Remember, an adjective is a 'describing' word.

Look carefully at Lowry's painting and answer the questions.

1 What can you see in the picture?

2 How do you think Lowry wanted his audience to feel about life in the town?

3 Make a list of adjectives to describe the picture.

4 Look at the two women to the left of the picture in the foreground. They are standing between a boy and a woman with a pram. The women are facing each other, obviously having a conversation. Imagine you are one of them and you have just moved to the town. You are telling the other woman how you feel about living in the town. Write your conversation.

Sandra Street

Steve and his classmates live in the West Indies. They have been asked to write a composition about Sandra Street where their school is. Some of the members of the class who do not live in Sandra Street have been quite insulting about it. Steve, who does live in Sandra Street, is upset but it makes him look very closely at the street for the first time.

Mr Blades, the new teacher, was delighted with the compositions we wrote about Sandra Street. He read some aloud to the class. He seemed particularly pleased when he read what was written by one of the boys from the other side of the town.

'Sandra Street is dull and uninteresting,' the boy wrote. 'For one half of its length there are a few houses and a private school (which we go to) but the other half is nothing but a wilderness of big trees.' Mr Blades smiled from the corners of his mouth and looked at those of us who belonged to Sandra Street. 'In fact,' the boy wrote, 'it is the only street in our town that has big trees, and I do not think it is a part of our town at all because it is so far and so different from our other streets.'

The boy went on to speak of the gay attractions on the other side of the town, some of which, he said, Sandra Street could never dream of having. In his street, for instance, there was the savannah where they played football and cricket, but the boys of Sandra Street had to play their cricket in the road . . .

Yet the boy's composition was very truthful. Sandra Street was so different from the other streets beyond. Indeed, it came from the very quiet fringes and ran straight up to the forests. As it left the town there were a few houses and shops along it, and then the school, and after that there were not many more houses, and the big trees started from there until the road trailed off to the river that bordered the forests. During the day all would be very quiet, except perhaps for the voice of one neighbour calling to another, and if some evenings brought excitement to the schoolyard, these did very little to disturb the calmness of Sandra Street . . .

5

Dreamingly I gazed out of the window. I noticed how Sandra Street stood away from the profusion of houses. Indeed, it did not seem to belong to the town at all. It stood away, not proudly, but sadly, as if it wanted peace and rest. I felt all filled up inside. Not because of the town in the distance but because of this strange little road. It was funny, the things the boy had written; he had written in anger what I thought of now in joy. He had spoken of the pleasures and palaces on the other side of the town. He had said why they were his home sweet home. As I looked at Sandra Street, I, too, knew why it was my home sweet home. It was dull and uninteresting to him but it meant so much to me.

From *Sandra Street and Other Stories* by Michael Anthony

COMPREHENSION   Read the passage and answer the questions.

1   Suggest a different title for the passage.

2   The boy who wrote about Sandra Street obviously doesn't like it. Pick out the words and phrases in the passage which give the reader this impression.

3   Where does the narrator, Steve, live?

4   What is the 'other side of the town' like?

5   What does the narrator think of Sandra Street?

6   Find the word in the passage that gives the reader the clue that this is not a British town.

7   Both the narrator and the boy who wrote the composition see the same things in Sandra Street but they feel very differently about it. How do they feel? Why do you think their feelings are so different?

OBSERVING AND RECORDING

We tend to take for granted the things we see every day. We don't look very closely at our surroundings because we see them so often and are familiar with them. The narrator in 'Sandra Street' looked closely at the area where he lived because someone had written about it, pointing out all the things that were wrong with it.

▲ Write a detailed description of the area in which you live for a friend who has never visited you. Choose your words carefully so that your friend has a clear picture of the area. Before you begin, here are some things to think about:

- Do you live in a city, town, village or out in the country?
- What kinds of house are there in your area?
- Do you have shops, a cinema or a park nearby?
- Is your area quiet or very busy?
- Do you like living there?

You could start by writing down all the ideas that come to you when you think about where you live. This is called **brainstorming**. You can then write your ideas in a **word web** like this:

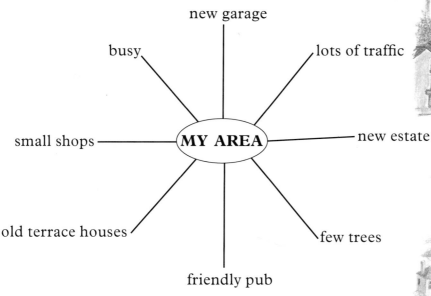

Remember:
Stage 1 – brainstorm
Stage 2 – make notes
Stage 3 – order your notes into paragraphs
Stage 4 – write a first draft
Stage 5 – proofread/revise – check spelling and punctuation.
          Does it give the right impression of where you live?
Stage 6 – present the final draft clearly and neatly.

Trip to London

By seven o'clock we were on our way
by train to London for the day,
four hours of travelling in the sun,
arrived in rain at Paddington
with neighbours, friends, mother and me,
and everyone had come to see
the big shops and the well-known sights,
the famous streets with all their lights.

Trafalgar Square

We strolled together everywhere,
fed pigeons in Trafalgar Square
who did not mind the drizzle there,
watched snorting traffic whizzing by,
waved at old Nelson standing high,
then sloshed our way to Waterloo
and, after lunch, went to the Zoo;
we managed to spend half an hour
learning history at the Tower
and just had time to see Hyde Park,
Buckingham Palace through the dark,
and going back I fell asleep
having no need for counting sheep.

We got back home at half-past eleven
and glad I was but still thanked heaven
for all I'd done and all I'd seen
though wished that I had met the Queen,
but never once shall I forget
slopping round London in the wet,
glad to be back with country things,
the trees and hills and murmurings
of bees in fields, birds on trees,
and rambling free and at my ease
whether in sun or whirling snow,
and all the people whom I know.

Leonard Clark

Tower of London from Tower Hill

Buckingham Palace

Nelson's Column

COMPREHENSION

Read the poem and answer the questions.

1 What impression does the poet give of London?

2 What does he think of the countryside?

3 What does the poet think is the main difference between the city and the countryside?

4 The rhythm the poet has used means that you can read the poem quickly. What impression does this give you of the trip to London?

RESEARCH

Many people visit London every year as there is so much to see there.

1 Make a list of the places the poet visits in *Trip to London*.

2 Choose two of them and write a descriptive paragraph about each.

Remember:
- use reference books and encyclopedias to research information
- make notes
- order your notes into paragraphs
- write your first draft
- proofread and revise – is it a clear description?
- present your final draft clearly and neatly.

PERSONAL CHOICE

Ask your teacher for a photocopy of the 'personal choice sheet'.

Choose one or two of the following assignments:

1 Write about the advantages and disadvantages of living in a city.

2 Places are often very different on a Sunday from other days in the week. Describe your area on a Sunday and show how it differs from other days.

3 Write a story called 'Moving House'. You can base this on your own experience or it can be imaginary. An important part of the story will be your first impressions of the area into which you have moved.

Remember the things to make notes on when you are writing a story:

- setting
- characters
- plot
- story beginning
- story ending

4 Make a Fact File on Lowry.

Victorian times

CHARACTERS IN STORIES

Authors have to let their readers know what sort of person each character is in their story.

- The author can describe the character.
- The reader can learn about the character by what he or she says and does.

In the following extracts from *A Christmas Carol* by Charles Dickens we learn a lot about a character called Scrooge.

Scrooge and Marley were partners in running a warehouse. At the beginning of the story Marley has died and Scrooge is described in detail.

Oh! But he was a tight-fisted hand at the grindstone, Scrooge! a squeezing, wrenching, grasping, scraping, clutching, covetous, old sinner! Hard and sharp as flint, from which no steel had ever struck out generous fire; secret, and self-contained, and solitary as an oyster.

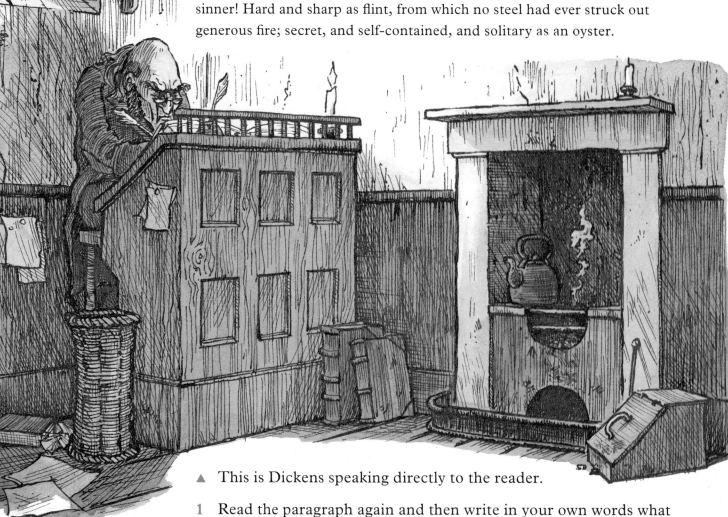

▲ This is Dickens speaking directly to the reader.

1 Read the paragraph again and then write in your own words what sort of person you think Scrooge is.

It is Christmas Eve and Scrooge's nephew comes to visit him.

"A merry Christmas, uncle! God save you!" cried a cheerful voice. It was the voice of Scrooge's nephew, who came upon him so quickly that this was the first intimation he had of his approach.

"Bah!" said Scrooge, "Humbug!" . . .

"Christmas a humbug, uncle!" said Scrooge's nephew. "You don't mean that, I am sure?"

"I do," said Scrooge. "Merry Christmas! What right have you to be merry? What reason have you to be merry? You're poor enough."

"Come then," returned the nephew, gaily. "What right have you to be dismal? What reason have you to be morose? You're rich enough."

Scrooge having no better answer ready on the spur of the moment, said, "Bah!" again, and followed it up with "Humbug!"

"Don't be cross, uncle!" said the nephew.

"What else can I be," returned the uncle, "when I live in such a world of fools as this? Merry Christmas! Out upon merry Christmas! What's Christmas time to you but a time for paying bills without money; a time for finding yourself a year older, and not an hour richer . . . If I could work my will," said Scrooge, indignantly, "every idiot who goes about with 'Merry Christmas' on his lips, should be boiled with his own pudding, and buried with a stake of holly through his heart. He should!"

From *A Christmas Carol* by Charles Dickens

2   In your own words write what you have learned about the sort of character Scrooge is from his conversation with his nephew.

The Water Babies

Tom is a rough and dirty chimney-sweep's apprentice who leads a miserable life. One day he runs away from his cruel master and then his adventures begin. Here is the opening of the story . . .

Once upon a time there was a little chimney-sweep, and his name was Tom . . . He lived in a great town in the North country, where there were plenty of chimneys to sweep, and plenty of money for Tom to earn and his master to spend. He could not read nor write, and did not care to do either; and he never washed himself, for there was no water up the court where he lived. He had never been taught to say his prayers . . . He cried half his time, and laughed the other half. He cried when he had to climb the dark flues, rubbing his poor knees and elbows raw; and when the soot got into his eyes, which it did every day in the week; and when his master beat him, which he did every day in the week; and when he had not enough to eat, which happened every day in the week likewise. And he laughed the other half of the day, when he was tossing halfpennies with the other boys, or playing leap-frog over the posts, or bowling stones at the horses' legs as they trotted by, which last was excellent fun, when there was a wall at hand behind which to hide. As for chimney-sweeping, and being hungry, and being beaten, he took all that for the way of the world . . .

Charles Kingsley

COMPREHENSION   Read the passage and answer the questions.

1   In your own words write what you have learned about Tom.

2   Have you learned about Tom through

   what the author has told you

   OR   what Tom has said himself?

Charles Dickens and Charles Kingsley lived in Victorian times but Leon Garfield is a modern writer who uses Victorian London as a setting for his books.

Smith

Smith is a twelve-year-old boy who lives by stealing. He has robbed an old man of a document. Two men later kill the old man while searching for the document, so Smith realises how important it is. Smith cannot read but he is sure the document will make his fortune so he wanders the streets of London trying to find someone who will teach him to read. Eventually he comes to St Andrew's Church.

'What d'you want, my child?'

A priest was in the pulpit, still as a carven saint.

'Oh, it's beautiful!' said Smith, ingratiatingly. 'Just like me sisters' stories of heaven!'

The priest nodded and smiled kindly.

'What are you looking for, my child?'

'Guidance, Your Reverence,' said Smith, who'd decided, this time, to ask roundabout.

'Are you lost?'

'Oh no, Your Worship! This is 'olborn 'ill!'

The priest compressed his lips and eyed Smith shrewdly. Hurriedly, Smith went on, 'Learn me to read, Your 'oliness. That's what I come for. Learn me to read so's I can read the 'oly Scripture.'

The priest stared in amazement at the filthy, strong-smelling little creature who stood in the aisle with his black hands pressed to his grubby heart.

'If you come and stand by the door during Service, then you'll hear me reading from the Holy Scripture, child. Won't that be a comfort and help?'

'Oh yes, Your Grace. And I'm humbly obliged. But what of when I'm 'ome – all in dirt and disorder? Who'll read to me then?

And me two poor sisters – a-panting, a-groaning, a-supplicating for salvation? Who'll read to them? Oh no, Your Reverence – I got to learn to read so's I can comfort meself in the dark o' the night . . . and light a little lamp in me sisters' souls with perusings aloud from the Good Book!'

But this was too much.

'You're a little liar!' exclaimed the priest, abruptly. Smith gazed thoughtfully up at him, proud in his white surplice and bands.

'And you're a fat bag of rotting flour!' he snarled suddenly. 'I 'ope the weevils gets you!'

Leon Garfield

COMPREHENSION

Read the passage and answer the questions.

1 What sort of man do you think the priest is? Give reasons for your answers.

2 What do you learn about Smith and how?

3 Design a 'Wanted' poster for Smith. The author has given you some idea of what he looks like. Write a description of Smith's character on the poster.

YOUR OWN CHARACTERS

A writer lets the reader know about the characters in the story by:
● describing them – speaking directly to the reader
● letting the reader learn about the character from what he or she says and does.

1 Write a description of a postwoman. Describe:
   ● what she looks like
   ● what sort of person she is. You must decide if she is cheerful, bad-tempered, serious and so on.

2 Your postwoman now delivers a parcel to a house. She has to knock on the door very early in the morning. Let the reader know what sort of person opens the door by what the character says and does. Write a conversation between the character and the postwoman.
   Read the following notes to help you plan your writing.

▲ Write notes on:
   the postwoman
   the person who opens the door
   their conversation.

▲ Think about how many paragraphs you will need:

paragraph 1 – description of the postwoman
paragraph 2 – the postwoman arriving at the door and knocking
paragraph 3 – the person opening the door and talking to the postwoman
paragraph 4 – the postwoman leaving.

This is just a suggestion – you may have your own ideas.

▲ Write your first draft.

▲ Proofread/revise. Think carefully about the words you have used.
Do they tell the reader what your characters are like?
Use a thesaurus to help you find more interesting words.
Look for spelling and punctuation mistakes.

▲ Present your final draft clearly and neatly.

PERSONAL CHOICE

Charles Dickens

Choose one of the following assignments:

1   Charles Dickens was a famous Victorian writer. Find out what you can about him and write the information in paragraphs. Remember the stages for factual writing:

stage 1 – research   **stage 4** – writing a first draft

stage 2 – making notes   **stage 5** – proofreading/revising

stage 3 – ordering your notes   **stage 6** – present the final draft

2   In *The Water Babies* Charles Kingsley writes about young boys climbing chimneys to clean them. Do you think this really happened or has the author made it up? Give reasons for your answer.

3   Smith did not succeed in getting the priest to teach him to read. Write about Smith meeting another character who will teach him.

The reader already knows about Smith but you must describe the new character and let the reader know what sort of person he or she is by what they say and do.

▲ Plan your story first:

● **plot** – what is going to happen between Smith and the new character?

● **setting** – where will the meeting take place?

● **characters** – what is the new character like? How does he/she treat Smith? What does he/she say and do?

Do you believe in ghosts?

In Penelope Lively's The Ghost of Thomas Kempe *Mr and Mrs Harrison and their children, James and Helen, move into an old cottage across the road from an elderly widow called Mrs Verity. No one knows that the cottage is haunted but James is made aware of the presence of Thomas Kempe, a seventeeth-century sorcerer who wants to make James his apprentice. Bert Ellison, the local handyman, is quite convinced of James's story and agrees to help him get rid of the ghost.*

He was rolling up the rug from the centre of the floor, and pushing back the table.

'What are you doing?' said James nervously.

'We've got to clear space for the circle, haven't we? What would your mother say to the odd chalk mark on the floor, do you think?'

'I don't think she'd be very pleased.'

'Well, we'd better not go causing trouble, I suppose. We'll have to make do with paper and pencil, though it should be chalk, properly speaking.' He delved in his overall pocket, and brought out a pencil, and then an envelope and contents which he was about to tear into pieces when he looked more closely and said, 'No. That's my football coupon, I'll be wanting that.'

'I've got some paper,' said James.

'Let's have it then.'

Bert tore a sheet of paper into eight pieces, sat down at the table, and pencilled on each one a series of indecipherable marks and scrawls, breathing heavily as he did so.

'What do they mean?' said James.

'Ah,' said Bert, 'now you're asking me. I had them from my dad, to tell the truth. He did a bit in this line, from time to time. I couldn't exactly tell you what they mean, but they've been known to work, and that's a fact.'

He placed the eight pieces of paper in a circle in the centre of the floor, weighting each one down with a nail from his toolbox. In the middle of the circle he put the forked rowan stick, propped against a chair. Then he walked over to the curtains, peered up at the top of them, and said, 'Drat it, these has got some sort of modern nonsense. It's the old-fashioned kind we need.'

'What?' said James, bewildered.

'A curtain ring, son. We need a brass curtain ring. Can you fix us up with one of them?'

'I 'spect so,' said James. He bolted down the stairs, dashed into the sitting-room, rummaged in his mother's work-drawer, found what he was looking for . . .

Bert placed the curtain ring over the pointed end of the stick, so that it slipped down the fork. Then he stepped away from the circle, motioned James back with his hand, cleared his throat loudly and said, 'Thomas Kempe! Are you there?'

James, who had not expected such a direct approach, was startled . . .

Nothing happened. Bert coughed, adjusted one of the pieces of paper and said, 'Enter the circle, and let us speak with you. Come!'

'What happens if he does?' whispered James.

'It'll do for him. The rowan, see. Rowan's no good for chaps like him. But you got to get him in there first.' Downstairs, a door banged, and somewhere outside Tim was barking.

'Thomas Kempe! I summon you!' said Bert severely. One of the pieces of paper lifted at the edge, as though examined by a curious breeze. There was a creak, that might or might not have been the shifting of ancient timbers. Bert said, in a murmur, 'He's biting! No doubt about it. This is where we got to go carefully. You've got to play them like a fish at this stage, see.' . . .

Down below, the front gate clicked and someone came up the path.

'Your mum?' said Bert.

'No,' said James. Footsteps are like voices, instantly known. 'It'll be someone collecting or something. Helen'll go.' He was staring at the rowan stick: was it moving, quivering just a little?

'You have a word with him,' said Bert. 'After all, it's you seem to have set him off in the first place.'

The last time I did that, thought James, it didn't turn out very well . . . With his eyes riveted on the stick (surely the ring twitched just then?) he said diffidently, 'Are you there?'

The stick shook. One of the nails rolled off its piece of paper.

'Ah,' said Bert. 'Go on.'

'Please could I talk to you?' said James more confidently. A small fist of air wandered across the back of his neck and the stick shook again, nudging the back of the chair. Downstairs, the front door opened and closed. There were voices in the hall—Helen and somebody else, but he hadn't time to listen. 'You're doing fine,' said Bert. 'Carry on like this and I'll be out of a job.'

'I wanted to ask you . . .' said James intensely, and the stick rubbed up and down again and the ring caught a strip of sunlight and flashed at him. The voices were louder.

'I wanted to ask if . . .' and then suddenly the voices were on the landing below and coming up the stairs and it was Helen and Mrs Verity and Mrs Verity was saying '. . . so if you don't mind dear I'll just pop up and have a word with him while he's here.'

The stick fell over with a clatter. The curtains bellied out into the room as the window burst open under a roll of air pressure. Mrs Verity and Helen came in as Bert was kicking the stick hastily under the bed and sweeping up the pieces of paper in one hand.

From *The Ghost of Thomas Kempe* by Penelope Lively

COMPREHENSION

Read the passage and answer the questions.

1 We are told that James 'nervously' asked Bert what he was doing. Can you think of two reasons why James would be nervous?

2 What things does Bert need to get rid of the ghost?

3 Why does Bert want Thomas Kempe to enter the circle?

4 What does Bert mean when he says, 'You got to play them like a fish at this stage'?

5 Find words in the passage that are closest in meaning to:

wrote　　searched　　surprised　　stared intensely

WRITING A GHOST STORY

The purpose of a ghost story is to frighten the reader. The reader doesn't want to be too scared but people do get enjoyment out of being just a little frightened.

The Ghost of Thomas Kempe shows one way of writing a ghost story. This way is by contrasting ordinary things with very unusual things.

	Ordinary	Unusual
CHARACTERS	Bert James Helen Mrs Verity	Thomas Kempe

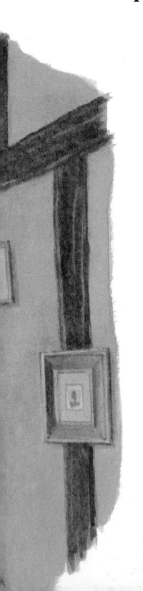

	Ordinary	Unusual
SETTING	the village James's house	mysterious atmosphere in James's room

PLOT	Bert finding his
	    football coupon
	someone coming to the
	    house
	the front door opening
	    and closing
	Mrs Verity and Helen
	    coming into the room
		marks and scrawls on paper
		    in a circle
		
		the rowan stick
		
		the breeze
		
		the window bursting open

The suspense is built up because we do not know if Bert and James will succeed in getting Thomas Kempe to appear before they are interrupted by people who are going about their ordinary business and know nothing of what is going on in James's room.

▲ Write your own ghost story using this method of contrast.
You can make a list like the one above to sort out the unusual things that are going to happen in your story and the ordinary things that happen.

▲ Brainstorm your ideas, and remember to:
- make notes on setting, character and plot (including beginning and ending);
- work out what is to happen in each paragraph;
- write a first draft; proofread and revise it carefully;
- think of an interesting title;
- present your final draft.

Two's Company

The sad story of a man who didn't believe in ghosts.

They said the house was haunted, but
He laughed at them and said, 'Tut, tut!
I've never heard such tittle-tattle
As ghosts that groan and chains that rattle;
And just to prove I'm in the right,
Please leave me here to spend the night.'

They left him just as dusk was falling
With a hunchback moon and screech-owls calling.

But what is that? Outside it seemed
As if chains rattled, someone screamed!
Come, come, it's merely nerves, he's certain
(But just the same, he draws the curtain).
The stroke of twelve – but there's no clock!
He shuts the door and turns the lock
(Of course, he knows that no one's there,
But no harm's done by taking care!);
Someone's outside – the silly joker,
(He may as well pick up the poker!).
That noise again! He checks the doors,
Shutters the windows, makes a pause
To seek the safest place to hide –
(The cupboard's strong – he creeps inside).
'Not that there's anything to fear!'
He tells himself, when at his ear
A voice breathes softly, 'How do you do!
I am a ghost. Pray, who are you?'

Raymond Wilson

POETRY STUDY

This is a narrative poem which tells the story of a man who didn't believe in ghosts. It shows a different way of writing a ghost story.

In the poem nothing ordinary happens. The writer builds up the suspense by having lots of very unusual things happen, which creates a frightening atmosphere. The man who didn't believe in ghosts gets more and more frightened.

1 Make a list of all the unusual things in the poem. The first few are done for you.

Unusual things

hunchback moon
screech-owls calling

2 Write a description of being alone in a haunted house. If a ghost appears it should happen at the end of your description. Concentrate on building up a frightening atmosphere by describing the unusual things that happen.

PERSONAL CHOICE

Choose one or two of the following assignments:

1 Imagine you are Thomas Kempe. You are in the room all the time Bert and James are planning to get rid of you. Write about how you feel and what you think of what they are doing.

2 The man in the poem *Two's Company* did not believe in ghosts. Do you believe in ghosts? Write about why you are convinced that ghosts exist or why you do not believe in them.

3 Have you ever had a ghostly experience – strange noises that you could find no reason for, things going missing without any reasonable explanation? Write about your experiences.

Other worlds

Tom has to go and stay with his Aunt Gwen and his Uncle Alan because his brother has measles. His aunt and uncle live in a first floor flat in an old house with no garden. One night, Tom hears the grandfather clock striking thirteen and he gets up to investigate. He looks out of the back door which leads on to a tiny yard . . .

Tom opened the door wide and let in the moonlight. It flooded in, as bright as daylight – the white daylight that comes before the full rising of the sun. The illumination was perfect, but Tom did not at once turn to see what it showed him on the clock-face. Instead he took a step forward on to the doorstep. He was staring, at first in surprise, then with indignation, at what he saw outside. That they should have deceived him – lied to him – like this! They had said, 'It's not worth your while going out at the back, Tom.' So carelessly they had described it: 'A sort of back-yard, very poky, with rubbish bins. Really, there's nothing to see.'

Nothing . . . Only this: a great lawn where flower-beds bloomed; a towering fir-tree, and thick, beetle-browed yews that humped their shapes down two sides of the lawn; on the third side, to the right, a greenhouse almost the size of a real house; from each corner of the lawn, a path that twisted away to some other depths of the garden, with other trees.

Tom had stepped forward instinctively, catching his breath in surprise; now he let his breath out in a deep sigh. He would steal out here tomorrow, by daylight. They had tried to keep this from him, but they could not stop him now – not his aunt, nor his uncle . . .

The scene tempted him even now: it lay so inviting and clear before him – clear-cut from the stubby leaf-pins of the nearer yew-trees to the curled-back petals of the hyacinths in the crescent-shaped corner beds. Yet Tom remembered his ten hours and his honour. Regretfully he turned from the garden, back indoors to read the grandfather clock.

He re-crossed the threshold, still absorbed in the thought of what he had seen outside. For that reason, perhaps, he could not at once make out how the hall had become different: his eyes informed him of some shadowy change; his bare foot was trying to tell him something . . .

The grandfather clock was still there, anyway, and must tell him the true time. It must be either twelve or one: there was no hour between. There is no thirteenth hour.

Tom never reached the clock with his inquiry, and may be excused for forgetting, on this occasion, to check its truthfulness. His attention was distracted by the opening of a door down the hall – the door of the ground-floor front flat. A maid trotted out.

From *Tom's Midnight Garden* by Philippa Pearce

COMPREHENSION   Read the passage and answer the questions.

1 Why was Tom out of bed so late at night?

2 Why did Tom think that his aunt and uncle had deceived him?

3 What is meant when the writer says that Tom would 'steal out' into the garden tomorrow?

4 What do you think 'his bare foot' was trying to tell him?

5 What do you think had happened when the clock struck thirteen?

STORIES IN OTHER WORLDS

Tom discovered a world set in a past time when
the grandfather clock struck thirteen.

1   With careful planning use this idea to write a short story
    of your own. You will need to think about the following:

Setting

This is probably the most important aspect of this type
of story. You need to choose a past time that you know
something about so that you can describe the setting in detail.

- Choose a time you have studied in history.

- Think about where your story is going to take place:

  a busy street scene
  inside a house
  at some historical event, for example the Fire of
      London, the Battle of Waterloo.

- What details will you describe? Be careful you don't
  have a car going down a street in Tudor times or
  cave people looking up at an aeroplane, as in this picture!

Characters

- Do you meet and talk with people from this past time?
- How do they react to you?
- How do you react to finding yourself in this strange situation?

Plot

- Tom was taken back into the past when the grandfather clock
  struck thirteen. How do **you** get into the past?

- What happens? Remember you are writing a short story so keep it simple.
  Decide on one thing that happens to you rather than lots of adventures.

- How do you get back to your own time?

- ▲ Make notes on setting, characters and plot.
  Work out what is going to happen in each paragraph.
  Write your first draft.
  Proofread/revise it carefully.
  Think of an interesting title for your story.

2   Present your final draft.

The Snow Spider

When Gwyn was five his sister Bethan mysteriously disappeared. The story opens on Gwyn's ninth birthday when he is given some unusual gifts by his grandmother. He is given a piece of seaweed, the yellow scarf Bethan was wearing when she disappeared, a tin whistle, a twisted metal brooch and a small broken horse. His grandmother says it is time to find out if Gwyn is a magician. He is to give the gifts to the wind and see what happens. Gwyn gives the brooch first and in return comes Arianwen, the snow spider. One day he sees Arianwen climbing up the back of an armchair . . .

When she reached the top she swung down to the arm, leaving a silver thread behind her. Up she went to the top again, and then down, her silk glistening in the firelight. Now the spider was swinging and spinning back and forth across the chair so fast that Gwyn could only see a spark, shooting over an ever-widening sheet of silver.

'A cobweb!' he breathed.

And yet it was not a cobweb. There was someone there. Someone was sitting where the cobweb should have been. A girl with long pale hair and smiling eyes: Bethan, sitting just as she used to sit, with her legs tucked under her, one hand resting on the arm of the chair, the other supporting her chin as she gazed into the fire. And still Arianwen spun, tracing the girl's face, her fingers and her hair, until every feature became so clear Gwyn felt he could have touched the girl.

The tiny spider entwined the silk on one last corner and then ceased her feverish activity. She waited, just above the girl's head, allowing Gwyn to contemplate her creation without interruption.

Was the girl an illusion? An image on a silver screen? No, she was more than that.

Gwyn could see the impression her elbow made on the arm of the chair, the fibres in her skirt, the lines on her slim, pale hand.

Only Bethan had ever sat thus. Only Bethan had gazed into the fire in such a way. But his sister was dark, her cheeks were rosy, her skin tanned golden by the wind. This girl was fragile and so silver-pale she might have been made of gossamer.

'Bethan?' Gwyn whispered, and he stretched out his hand towards the girl.

A ripple spread across the shining image, as water moves when a stone pierces the surface, but Gwyn did not notice a cool draught entering the kitchen as the door began to open.

'Bethan?' he said again.

The figure shivered violently as the door swung wider, and then the light went on. The girl in the cobweb hovered momentarily and gradually began to fragment and to fade until Gwyn was left staring into an empty chair.

Jenny Nimmo

COMPREHENSION

Read the passage and answer the questions.

1 What words does the writer use to describe how Gwyn speaks? Why does she use these words instead of 'said'?

2 What evidence made Gwyn believe that Bethan was more than an illusion?

3 In what ways was the girl in the cobweb the same as his sister Bethan? In what ways was she different?

VISITORS FROM OTHER WORLDS

In *Tom's Midnight Garden* Tom has contact with another world when he finds himself in a past time.

In *The Snow Spider* Gwyn has contact with another world when Bethan visits his world.

▲ Imagine that Gwyn and Bethan were not interrupted at this point in the story. Bethan is able to tell her brother about the other world that she has disappeared into.

▲ Write their conversation, giving a detailed description of this 'other world'. The poem on the opposite page might help you. It was written by Kelly Williams of Deighton Primary School, Tredegar, Gwent. Kelly's class had read the whole book.

The other world

First a silver web,
Shimmering and shining,
Then another world.
A pure white tower
With a silver bell at the top,
Gleaming in a ray of moonlight,
Sparkling and glistening.
Silver leaves dangling on the trees
And icicles singing in the breeze.
A world drained of colour
But full of enchantment.
Pale children with arctic eyes and silver hair,
Ethereal and serene,
Laughing and singing
In sweet delicate voices.
A silver ship
Floating noiselessly through the sky,
The sails like silver cobwebs,
Glistening and mysterious
And the children onboard
Singing and dancing to haunting music.

Kelly Williams

PERSONAL CHOICE

Choose one of the following assignments:

1   Make a book cover for *Tom's Midnight Garden* or
    The Snow Spider. You will need to:

- write the title and the author on the front cover.

- draw a picture that gives the reader some idea of
  what the book is about.

- write a book blurb for the back cover.

2   Gwyn's grandmother gives him the strange gifts to see if
    he is a magician. Imagine you are Gwyn and write a diary
    extract for the day you receive the gifts and for the day you
    see Bethan in the cobweb.

27

Advertising

Advertisements surround us in our daily lives – on the television, on hoardings, in newspapers and magazines. Everywhere, we are faced with words and pictures that are trying to persuade us that we really need to buy certain things to be healthy, happy and comfortable.

Let's look at how some of these advertisements work!

Look carefully at the advertisement on the opposite page and answer the questions.

1 What is the advertisement selling?

2 Who is the advertisement aimed at?

3 What is the name of the cereal trying to tell you?

4 Make a list of the words in the advertisement that are used to persuade you to buy it.

5 Why does the advertisement tell you that 'all good supermarkets' stock this cereal?

6 Why do you think the advertiser has used the rhyme 'the healthy way to start your day'?

7 Would you buy this product?

a If you would buy it then the advertisement has been successful as far as you are concerned. Explain the reasons why it has persuaded you to buy **Supermunch**.

OR

b If you would not buy this cereal then the advertisement has been unsuccessful as far as you are concerned. Explain the reasons why you would not buy the product.

29

People who write advertisements are trying to persuade you to buy the product.

They make an advertisement attractive and eye-catching so you will stop and look at it.

What does it look like?
Advertisers think carefully about what an advertisement looks like and who it is aimed at. They consider:

- **colour**
  use of bright colours
  use of black and white
  use of colours that blend together
  use of colours that contrast

- **layout**
  clear, easy to read
  busy, lots going on
  name of product very obvious

- **illustration**
  drawings
  photographs
  diagrams

What does it tell you?

- **persuasive language**
  The advertiser makes you feel that you really **need** this product. It isn't just good, it is **fantastic**. It isn't just helpful, it is a **miracle worker**!

- **rhyming slogans**
  These are often used because they will stick in your mind.
  ▲ Which of the following slogans is more memorable?

Supermunch is a good cereal

OR

Supermunch – the healthy way to start your day

- **information**
  what it can do for you
  why you really need it
  price
  where you can buy it.

WRITING ADVERTISEMENTS

Look at the pictures below:

▲ Choose two of the products and design a magazine advertisement for each of them.
Plan your advertisement by making notes on the following before you begin:

- a name for the product
- who it is aimed at
- how you will make it eye-catching
- what language you will use to persuade people to buy the product.

Look carefully at these advertisements from around 1916.
Write a short report on one of them, saying how successful
you think it might have been and why. Remember to plan your
report by making notes on the following:

- what product is being advertised

- who the advertisement is aimed at

- how eye-catching it is

- how persuasive is the language used

- how much information it gives

- how memorable it is.

▲ Find a modern advertisement that is about the same type of thing
and compare the two. Here are some things to help you:

- which is more eye-catching?

- which is more persuasive?

- which gives you more information?

- which are you more likely to remember?

PERSONAL CHOICE

Choose one or two of the following assignments:

1. Think of an advertisement you have seen that has persuaded you or someone in your family to buy the product. Write about why the advertisement had this effect on you.

2. Think of an advertisement you have seen recently that has annoyed you. Explain why it had this effect on you.

3. Advertisements are aimed at different audiences. Look through newspapers and magazines and find an advertisement aimed at:

   - a young person
   - a person who is concerned about staying healthy
   - a person who likes fast, luxurious cars

   For each advertisement explain how you know it is aimed at this particular audience.

4. Choose an item you have at home that you are really pleased with. Write an advertisement for it to persuade other people to buy it.

The unsinkable *Titanic*

The Titanic

*Here are **two** accounts detailing some of the events during the sinking of the* Titanic. *The first is by someone who was actually there, the second is written by a reporter who interviewed a surviving passenger.*

As the tilt grew steeper, the forward funnel toppled over. It struck the water on the starboard side with a shower of sparks and a crash heard above the general uproar . . . The *Titanic* was now absolutely perpendicular. From the third funnel aft, she stuck straight up in the air, her three dripping propellers glistening even in the darkness . . . Out in the boats, they could hardly believe their eyes. For over two hours they had watched, hoping against hope, as the *Titanic* sank lower and lower. When the water reached her red and green running lights, they knew the end was near . . . but nobody dreamed it would be like this – the unearthly din, the black hull hanging at ninety degrees, the Christmas-card backdrop of brilliant stars . . . Two minutes passed, the noise finally stopped, and the *Titanic* settled back slightly at the stern. Then slowly she began sliding under, moving at a steep slant. As she glided down, she seemed to pick up speed. When the sea closed over the flagstaff on her stern, she was moving fast enough to cause a slight gulp.

From *A Night to Remember* by Walter Lord

COMPREHENSION

Read the first-hand account before writing the answers.

1 What do you think caused the 'general uproar' on the ship?

2 What does the writer mean when he says the ship was 'absolutely perpendicular'?

3 What adjective does the writer use to describe the propellers? Why?

4 What were the people in the boats 'hoping against hope' would not happen?

5 Explain in your own words 'the Christmas-card backdrop of brilliant stars'.

6 Explain the meaning of these words. Use a dictionary to help you:

starboard   aft   hull   flagstaff

Mr C.H. Stengel, a first-class passenger, said that when the *Titanic* struck the iceberg the impact was terrific, and great blocks of ice were thrown on the deck, killing a number of people. The stern of the vessel rose in the air, and people ran shrieking from their berths below. Women and children, some of the former naturally hysterical, having been rapidly separated from husbands, brothers and fathers, were quickly placed in boats by the sailors, who like their officers, it was stated, were heard by some survivors to threaten men that they would shoot if male passengers attempted to get in the boats ahead of the women. Indeed, it was said that shots were actually heard. Mr Stengel added that a number of men threw themselves into the sea when they saw that there was no chance of their reaching the boats. "How they died," he observed, "I do not know." He dropped overboard, caught hold of the gunwale of a boat, and was pulled in because there were not enough sailors to handle her. In some of the boats women were shrieking for their husbands; others were weeping, but many bravely took a turn at the oars.

Daily Herald, 22nd April 1912

COMPREHENSION

Read this reporter's account of what a surviving passenger said and answer the questions.

1 What does the reporter mean when he says that Mr Stengel was a 'first-class passenger'?

2 Why were women and children put into the lifeboats first?

3 How do you know that some of the male passengers tried to get into the lifeboats before the women and children?

4 Why was Mr Stengel pulled into the lifeboat?

5 How does the reporter convey the feeling of panic on the ship?

6 Explain the meanings of these words. Use a dictionary to help you:

berth   stern   gunwale

Both these accounts of the sinking of the *Titanic* were written for an audience. Their purpose was to inform people of the events of that terrible night.

Both Walter Lord and Mr Stengel actually experienced the catastrophe. The difference is that Walter Lord wrote about his experience **first-hand** whereas what Mr Stengel experienced was **reported** by someone else.

1   Read the two accounts again. There are certain phrases in the second account which show that the reporter was getting his facts second-hand, for example: 'Mr C.H. Stengel . . . said that . . .'

Can you find any more examples?

2   Imagine you were on the *Titanic* and you got into a lifeboat very quickly.

   a   Write a short account of what happened to you.

   b   Write the same account as if you were a reporter hearing it from someone else.

Remember:
research
making notes
ordering notes
writing a first draft
proofreading/revising
present the final draft.

RESEARCH

Use your answers to the following questions, and anything else you can find out, to write a short factual report on the sinking of the *Titanic*.

1   How many storeys high was the *Titanic*?

2   How long was she?

3   In which shipyard was she built?

4   Where did she sail from on her maiden voyage?

5   What was her destination?

6   How many passengers were on board?

7   How many crew were on board?

8   On what date and at what time was the *Titanic* struck by an iceberg?

9   How many lives were lost?

Morgan Robertson was an American writer who lived from 1861 to 1915. In 1900 he wrote a book called *Futility* about the biggest and grandest passenger liner ever built. She set sail from Southampton on her maiden voyage to America in 1898, but she never got there! The ship collided with an iceberg in the North Atlantic and sank with a terrible loss of life. The name of this fictional ship in Robertson's book was the *Titan*!

In 1892 a famous journalist, W T Stead, published a short story which predicted the sinking of the real *Titanic*. Twenty years later he was on the *Titanic*'s maiden voyage and died when the ship went down.

In April 1935 William Reeves, a young sailor, was on watch at the bow of a tramp steamer sailing from Tyneside to Canada. He knew all about April being a bad month for icebergs and he knew that the *Titanic* had been struck at midnight – the hour his watch was to end. He was very worried but was afraid to sound the alarm as his shipmates would make fun of him. He stared ahead into the gloom but could see nothing. Suddenly he remembered the exact date the *Titanic* went down – April 14th 1912 – this was also the day he was born! He shouted a warning and the helmsman stopped the boat only a few yards from an enormous iceberg. The crew soon realised that they were totally surrounded by icebergs and it took a Newfoundland ice-breaker nine days to smash its way through. The name of the tramp steamer was the *Titanian*.

All three extracts adapted from *The Reader's Digest Book of Strange Stories/Amazing Facts*

All these events are very strange. Read them again carefully and make notes on the following:

1 How many ways can you think of to explain how Robertson and Stead came to write their stories and how Reeves saved his ship from disaster?

2 What do you believe is the best explanation?

PERSONAL CHOICE   Choose one or two of the following assignments:

1 Imagine you are a survivor of the *Titanic* disaster. Write a letter to a close friend telling him or her what happened to you that night.

2 Imagine you interviewed Mr C H Stengel shortly after his ordeal on the *Titanic*. Decide what questions you would ask him and write them out with his responses, for example:

Interviewer: What were you doing when the *Titanic* hit the iceberg?

Mr Stengel: I was asleep in my stateroom.

3 Icebergs have always been hazardous for ships.
Find out the following:

   a How much of an iceberg is above the water and how much below?

   b What kind of water is an iceberg made of?

   c Which is the largest iceberg ever recorded?

   d Which is the tallest iceberg ever recorded?

   e What is the furthest an Arctic iceberg has ever drifted?

▲ Draw a picture of an iceberg and write the facts you have found out around it. Make it a clear and attractive way of presenting your information.

39

Jamaica

Jamaica is a tropical paradise, an island of colour and warmth lying in the beautiful blue waters of the Caribbean. The spectacular Blue Mountains are ringed with lush forests, magical plantations and incredible beaches. Palm trees sway in the warm breezes and luxurious hotels stand side by side with thatched hut villages in welcoming resorts.

Jamaica is an island that offers holidays with something for everyone. If you are looking for an activity there are plenty of sports on offer — water sports on the beach, scuba diving, golf, to name but a few. If that sounds a bit too energetic then just relax in the warmth of the Caribbean sun and drink in the beautiful surroundings.

eight

Island Information

Old Plantation House

MONTEGO BAY · FALMOUTH · RUNAWAY BAY

OCHO RIOS · ORACABESSA · PORT MARIA

NEGRIL ·

JAMAICA

· KINGSTON

N

Capital: Kingston

Population: 2.4 million

Size: 4244 square miles

Currency: Jamaican $

Climate: Average temp. 84°F
May & October tropical thunderstorms

Health: No vaccinations necessary

Time difference: GMT 5 hours earlier

Temperatures

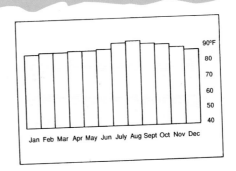

Transport

The local taxis are reasonably cheap and are a good way of getting about. Expect to pay about £10.00 for an 8 km journey.

Eating Out

You will find no shortage of places to eat. Choose from international cuisine or, for the more adventurous, local dishes such as conch!

Average rainfall

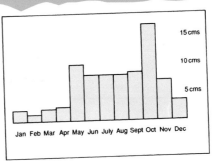

nine

Montego Bay

This is Jamaica's second city and main tourist resort. It is a busy, lively place, ideal for those looking for a fun-packed, entertaining holiday. Attractions include rafting trips on the Martha Brae and the famous Doctor's Cave Beach. ● ● ● ● ●

Doctor's Cave Beach

| 14 nights | Seaview Hotel | | | | | |
| Prices in £s per person | Hotel room | | | Self-catering | | |
No of people	4	3	2	4	3	2
1–19 May	439	469	559	449	499	599
20 May–2 June	459	489	589	469	519	629
3–23 June	459	489	589	479	529	639
24 June–7 July	489	539	629	519	579	679
8–21 July	499	549	639	529	589	689
22–28 July	549	579	699	589	629	759
29 July–18 August	579	629	729	619	679	789
19 August–1 September	549	579	689	579	619	739
2–15 September	499	549	639	529	589	689
16–29 September	479	529	619	509	569	663
30 Sept–20 October	459	489	589	479	529	639
21–31 October	459	489	589	479	529	639
1–8 November	429	459	549	449	489	599
9–24 November	399	439	529	429	469	569
25 Nov–4 December	379	419	499	399	449	549

ten

Ocho Rios

This is one of Jamaica's top resorts with crescent-shaped beaches lapped by turquoise seas and backed by lush green mountains. It is ideally situated for visits to the Shaw Park Botanical Gardens and the spectacular Dunn's River Falls — a cool waterfall tumbling over a natural stone stairway. It is a small holiday town with a friendly, relaxing atmosphere.

Dunn's River Falls

14 nights Prices in £s per person	Palms Hotel Hotel room		
No of people	4	3	2
1–19 May	429	459	529
20 May–2 June	449	479	549
3–23 June	459	489	559
24 June–7 July	489	519	589
8–21 July	499	539	609
22–28 July	569	599	669
29 July–18 August	599	629	699
19 Aug–1 September	559	589	659
2–15 September	499	529	599
16–29 September	479	499	579
30 Sept–20 October	459	479	559
21–31 October	469	489	569
1–8 November	399	439	499
9–24 November	379	419	479
25 Nov–4 December	369	399	459

eleven

COMPREHENSION

The pages from a travel brochure about Jamaica contain a lot of information in the form of text, pictures, charts and a map. You must look at all of the information very carefully to answer the following questions:

1 Where is Jamaica?

2 What can a holiday in Jamaica offer you?

3 What sort of scenery would you expect to find in Jamaica?

4 In which month is the highest rainfall?

5 Where is Jamaica's main international airport?

6 What is the capital of Jamaica?

7 What is the average temperature?

8 Is Falmouth on the north or south of the island?

9 In which resort could you have a self-catering holiday?

10 Which resort is situated near the Dunn's River Falls?

Negril Beach

WRITING TO PERSUADE

A holiday brochure is a good example of writing that is designed to persuade.

▲ Write a short report on how the pages on Jamaica persuade people to visit the island. You need to consider:

- the layout
- the use of vocabulary
- the illustrations
- how clearly the information is presented.

BOOKING YOUR HOLIDAY

There are many decisions to be made before you fill in a booking form for a holiday.

Imagine you are planning a two week holiday to Jamaica, staying in either Montego Bay or Ocho Rios. Make notes on the following:

1   How many people are going – 2, 3 or 4?

2   What sort of accommodation do you want?
   - hotel
   - self-catering

3   What dates do you want to be away?
   - when the prices are cheapest
   - during the school holidays
   - when you can avoid tropical rainstorms
   - when you can experience the tropical rainstorms
   - at the hottest time
   - at the coolest time

4   Do you have any special requirements?
   - vegetarian meals
   - room with a view of the sea
   - wheelchair access to room

▲ When you have made your notes you have to decide exactly when and where you are going. Sometimes you can't have everything you want, for example:
   - You may want to go when it is cheapest but you can only go in the school holidays.
   - You may want to avoid the tropical rainstorms but you can only go in May or October.
   - You may want to stay at Ocho Rios but you want a self-catering holiday.

▲ Get as many aspects of your holiday right as you can, then ask your teacher for a photocopy of the booking form and fill it in.

DID YOU HAVE A GOOD TIME?

On your return from your holiday in Jamaica you write a business letter to the travel company. Remember how to set out and write a business letter:

- **Your address** at the top right-hand side.

- **The date** under your address.

- **Address of the organisation/company** you are writing to at the left-hand side.

- **The greeting** – 'Dear Sir/Madam' if you do not know the name of the person.

- **Content of the letter** – keep it concise and to the point and be courteous.

- **Closing** – 'Yours faithfully' if you began 'Sir/Madam'. 'Yours sincerely' if you wrote to a person by name.

- **Your signature** and **your printed name**.

1 Imagine that you have had a wonderful time. The hotel/self-catering was excellent and everything that the brochure said about Jamaica was true. Write to the travel company congratulating them on providing a wonderful holiday.

2   Imagine that you did not have a good time. The accommodation was poor and the food awful. You had to queue for long periods of time to go rafting and on the water slide, and the scuba-diving was always fully booked. Write a letter to the travel company complaining that you were very disappointed and would not travel with them again.

PERSONAL CHOICE

Choose one or two of the following assignments:

1   Using what you have learnt about Jamaica, design a travel poster. The illustrations and text must make the audience want to go there. Look back at **Unit 5 – Advertising** to help you.

2   Imagine you are on holiday in Jamaica and have just had your first scuba-diving lesson. Write a letter to a friend back home describing your experience.

Remember:
name of product
audience
colour and layout
illustration
persuasive language
rhyming slogans

3   Do some research on the facts of Jamaica:

geography – industry, agriculture, mountains, rivers, etc.

history – when was it discovered, who lived there, who settled there, and so on.

▲   Make your notes into an information sheet or a wall display.

Night

Night Shapes

Outside is full of cats and darkness,
Howling screeches and thick black stillness,
Things creeping silently,
Bats shuddering restlessly,
Owls hooting,
Moles rooting.

Outside is full of black shapes moving,
Shadows weird and slowly passing,
Things watching the dark,
Eyes looking for work,
Figures stealing
Night brooding.

Outside is full of people dreaming,
Hoping, muttering, turning, scheming,
Ideas moving in the mind,
Voices uttering no sound
Time slipping,
Dawn looming.

Paddy Kinsale

COMPREHENSION   Read the poem and answer the questions.

1   What do 'thick black stillness', 'creeping silently' and
    'Shadows weird' tell you about the poet's attitude to night time?

2   What do you think are the 'Things watching the dark'?

3   What do you think the poet's attitude is to the people who are
    outside at night?

4   Explain the meaning of these verbs as the poet has used them in
    the poem:

    stealing   brooding   looming

Verbs are
sometimes called
'doing' words.

Night

Silently sleeps the river.
The dark pines hold their peace.
The nightingale does not sing,
Or the corncrake screech.

Night. Silence enfolds.
Only the brook murmurs,
And the brilliant moon turns
Everything to silver.

Silver the river,
And the rivulets.
Silver the grass
Of the fertile steppes.

Night. Silence enfolds.
All sleeps in Nature
And the brilliant moon
Turns everything to silver.

Sergei Esenin

COMPREHENSION   Read the poem and answer the questions.

1   What do 'Silently sleeps the river',
    'Silence enfolds' and 'brilliant moon' tell you
    about the poet's attitude to night time?

2   What do you think are the 'fertile steppes'?

3   What effect does the moonlight have on the landscape?

4   Which of the two poems on night do you prefer?
    Give your reasons.

POETRY AND PURPOSE

As with all kinds of writing, poetry has a purpose.
It may be to entertain, to give a message or to
make the reader see something very clearly.

Poetry is usually written from the personal viewpoint
of the poet. Look again at the two poems about night.
By looking carefully at the choice of words each poet has
used, the reader can tell what each poet's view of night is.

Night Shapes

This poem is full of menace and disturbing ideas. Look at the
words in the word web that the poet has chosen to describe the night:

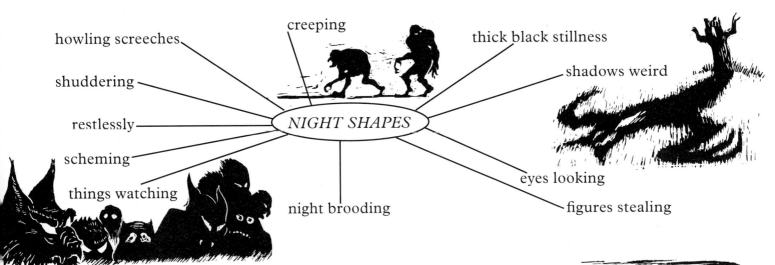

howling screeches
creeping
thick black stillness
shuddering
shadows weird
restlessly
NIGHT SHAPES
scheming
things watching
eyes looking
night brooding
figures stealing

Night

This poem gives you a sense of peace and beauty. Look at the words
in the word web that the poet has chosen to describe the night:

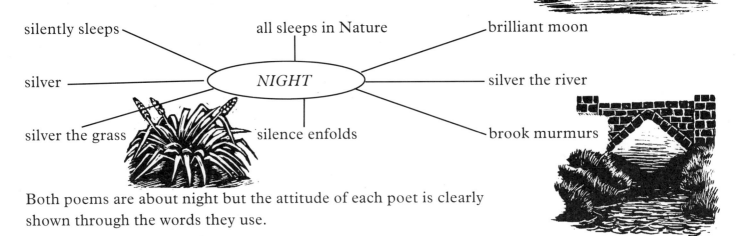

silently sleeps
all sleeps in Nature
brilliant moon
silver
NIGHT
silver the river
silver the grass
silence enfolds
brook murmurs

Both poems are about night but the attitude of each poet is clearly
shown through the words they use.

Paddy Kinsale sees the night as something threatening whereas
Sergei Esenin describes a peaceful, beautiful scene.

50

WRITING YOUR OWN NIGHT POEM

1 Things for you to think about:

Setting What scene are you going to describe at night?

- a busy street scene
- a deserted house
- the view from your window
- a railway station

Viewpoint How do you find the night?

- friendly
- frightening
- mysterious

2 Making a start:

a Start by listing all the nouns (including abstract nouns) that you are going to use in your poem. For instance, some of the concrete and abstract nouns in *Night Shapes* are:

cats   darkness   screeches   bats   owls   moles

stillness   shadows   shapes   figures   people

> Remember, **abstract nouns** denote qualities, feelings, times or actions which you can't see, touch, taste, smell or hear.

b Look at your list and add adjectives and verbs to describe each thing. The words you choose will show the reader what your view of night is. Paddy Kinsale chose some eerie, menacing **adjectives** and *verbs*:

night *brooding*
thick black stillness
shadows **weird**
bats *shuddering* restlessly
figures *stealing*
people *scheming*

The poem would have been very different if he had chosen different words, like:

soft screeches
warm peaceful stillness
shadows *dancing*
bats *gliding*
figures *strolling*
people *singing*

3 Now write your poem.

The Highwayman

This is the first stanza of a long poem by Alfred Noyes
in which he describes the night in vivid detail.

The wind was a torrent of darkness among the gusty trees,
The moon was a ghostly galleon tossed upon cloudy seas,
The road was a ribbon of moonlight over the purple moor,
And the highwayman came riding –
     Riding – riding –
The highwayman came riding, up to the old inn-door.
He'd a French cocked-hat on his forehead, a bunch of lace
     at his chin,
A coat of the claret velvet, and breeches of brown doeskin:
They fitted with never a wrinkle; his boots were up to the
     thigh!
And he rode with a jewelled twinkle,
     His pistol butts a-twinkle,
His rapier hilt a-twinkle, under the jewelled sky.

SIMILES AND METAPHORS

The poet describes the night scene by using **metaphors**. These are like similes but they do not say one thing is **like** or **as** another, they say one thing **is** or **was** another.

simile	metaphor
The wind was **like** a torrent of darkness.	The wind **was** a torrent of darkness.
The moon was **like** a ghostly galleon.	The moon **was** a ghostly galleon.
The road was **like** a ribbon of moonlight.	The road **was** a ribbon of moonlight.

▲ Write a simile and a metaphor for each of these:

shadows
stars
the night sky
street lights
bats flying at night.

PERSONAL CHOICE

Choose one or two of the following assignments:

1   Using *Night Shapes* as the setting, write a description of a walk home in the dark. Remember that the poet has made night disturbing and menacing and you must reflect this in your description.

2   How do you feel about night? Do you find it frightening or calm and peaceful? Write about your thoughts and feelings.

3   Continue the story of *The Highwayman*. Why is he riding to the inn at dead of night? What do you think happens when he arrives there?

You have the setting and the main character. You need to think about the plot and other characters you may need in the story.

Extinction!

The blue waters of the ocean were calm at dawn; its surface was like a liquid mirror. To the west, the cloudless sky was a deep, dark blue. But to the east, the sky had turned a shade lighter as the red morning sun began to rise over a thin strip of rough forestland in the distance. There, sheltered by a rocky bay, three boats waited to trap a killer whale.

Not far from the bay, a long, black dorsal fin knifed across the ocean surface. It was followed by another and then another, gliding in graceful arcs up and out and then back into the water. Gradually, the fins rose higher revealing the broad, slick backs of six whales blowing great bursts of misty spray through blow-holes as they broke the surface.

In the rocky bay, the biggest of the three boats, a ragged old brown fishing trawler, chugged slowly in a semicircle leaving a long rusted metal net in its wake. Once the metal net sank into the water, no living creature larger than a man's fist could swim through it.

A smaller, faster chase boat drifted quietly outside the bay. On the deck, its captain held a pair of binoculars to his weathered face. He had just spotted the tall, black dorsal fins of the whales slicing through the smooth waters towards him. He had been waiting two weeks for this moment. If he succeeded in catching a whale, he would soon earn enough money to buy a new boat. He was determined not to fail.

Swimming playfully through the water, the pod of six killer whales was unaware of the danger that lay ahead. The whales knew each other well. They had been together their entire lives. They had hunted and played together, rubbed each other's bellies with their long, rounded flippers, nursed their baby calves, and come to the aid of each other when they were sick or injured. They were as much a family as that of any two-legged creature who walked on land.

One of the whales was larger than a calf, but not yet fully grown. Like the others, he was jet-black with a gleaming white underbelly and a small white patch behind each eye. But this young whale had special markings that none of the others possessed – three small dark spots under his broad white jaw. So he was known as Three Spots.

As the whales glided through the cold, clear waters towards the rocky bay, Three Spots swam ahead, playfully racing in and out of thick fifty-foot-long ribbons of brownish-green kelp. On the deck of the chase boat, the captain could now see the whales quite clearly as they swam into the bay, unaware that they were surrounded on three sides by the curtain of steel netting.

'Now!' the captain shouted. The chase boat's engines fired up with a roar. In the water near by, the pod of swimming whales came to an abrupt halt. Instantly alert, they raced to the surface and poked their black heads out of the water, spy-hopping as they looked around for the source of the unpleasant noise.

What they saw terrified them. The chase boat was roaring towards them, trying to herd them deeper into the net. To confuse and frighten the whales, the men aboard the chase boat banged its hull with their hands and sticks of wood. Meanwhile the large brown trawler lumbered across the bay, pulling the net closed.

Sensing they were in danger, the pod of whales sped quickly towards the safety of the open ocean. It was a race now. Could the whales get out of the bay before the trawler pulled the net closed? The whales kicked their mighty tails as hard as they could. Ahead, through the clear water, they could see the hull of the trawler crossing in front of them as it pulled the net tighter.

There was still a small opening in the net and beyond it, the open ocean. The lead whale swam through. Then the second, third, fourth and fifth before the net shut behind them.

Outside the bay, the whales rejoiced in their freedom. They gathered together and spy-hopped, poking their massive heads out of the water and looking around to make sure they had all escaped.

Then they heard a long, mournful squeal. Trapped inside the net, Three Spots slowly circled as he searched in vain for a way out. But there was no way round the nets. Three Spots had been caught.

From *Free Willy* by Todd Strasser

COMPREHENSION   Read the passage and answer the questions.

1   Why does the writer say that the black dorsal fin of a whale 'knifed' across the ocean surface?

2   Why is the captain especially determined to catch a whale?

3 The writer explains how the whales behave, how they live together and how they help one another. What effect does he hope this will have on the reader?

4 What alerted the whales to the fact that they were in danger?

5 How did the men try to confuse and frighten the whales?

6 How did the other whales realise that Three Spots had been caught?

7 How do you, as the reader, react to the capture of Three Spots?

WRITING ABOUT VARIOUS OPINIONS

People have various opinions about whether it is right to hunt whales for profit.

▲ Write a report based on these opinions. You will need to plan your work in the following way.

Stage 1 – **Research**
Opinions are more convincing if they are based on **facts**. You will need to find out the facts of the case using reference books, newspapers, etc.

Stage 2 – **Making notes**
Once you have found your sources of information you will need to make notes on the important points. Here are some of the facts you would find out about whaling.

The whaling industry provides jobs for many people.

Some species of whales have been hunted so much that they are almost extinct.

Catching whales by harpooning is far more cruel than the slaughter of domestic land animals.

A dead whale is estimated as being worth about £10,000.

The Eskimos (Inuits) have always hunted the whale as part of their means of staying alive.

Laws have been passed to control how many whales are killed. If these laws are not obeyed then many species of whale will become extinct.

Stage 3 – Ordering your notes

Some of the facts will probably support the hunting of whales and some of the facts will be against the hunting of whales.

Whales provide meat and oil.

1   Copy these headings and put each fact under the right heading.

For hunting whales   *Against hunting whales*

By doing this you have the two main parts of your report.

There are about two million sperm whales and three to four million minke whales so they are in no danger of extinction.

2   You will now need an introduction
    so the reader knows what you are writing about.
    Choose one of the following
    to research for your introduction:

    - facts about the different types of whale

    - facts about how long whales have been hunted for profit.

3   You now need to think carefully about your **conclusion**.
    How are you going to end your report? Choose one of
    the following for your conclusion based on the facts:

    - whale hunting should be allowed to go on

    - whale hunting should be stopped

    - whale hunting should be allowed
      provided that the number of
      whales killed is controlled.

Stage 4 – Writing a first draft

Stage 5 – Proofreading/revising

Stage 6 – Present the final draft

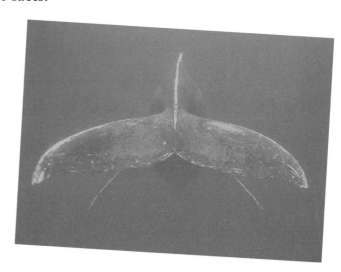

The Song of the Whale

Heaving mountain in the sea,
Whale, I heard you
Grieving.

Great whale, crying for your life,
Crying for your kind, I knew
How we would use
Your dying:

Lipstick for our painted faces,
Polish for our shoes.

Tumbling mountain in the sea,
Whale, I heard you
Calling.

Bird-high notes, keening, soaring:
At their edge a tiny drum
Like a heartbeat.

We would make you
Dumb.

In the forest of the sea,
Whale, I heard you
Singing,

Singing to your kind.
We'll never let you be.
Instead of life we choose

Lipstick for our painted faces,
Polish for our shoes.

Kit Wright

COMPREHENSION

Read the poem and answer the questions.

1. In your own words write what the poem is about.
2. Why is the whale 'crying' for its life and 'crying' for its 'kind'?
3. What have lipstick and polish got to do with the whale?
4. What does the poet mean when he says to the whale: 'We would make you dumb'?
5. For what purpose has the poet written this poem?
6. How does the poet want this poem to affect the reader?
7. Why do you think the poet has decided to put the words:

   grieving   calling   dumb   singing

   on separate lines?

PERSONAL CHOICE

Choose one or two of the following assignments:

1. Write an account of the capture of Three Spots from the point of view of one of the whales which escaped. Begin when the whales were playing in the water and were unaware that they were in great danger.
2. Design a poster which gives a clear message that you think either:
   - whale hunting should be allowed

   OR

   - whale hunting should be banned.
3. Choose another animal that is in danger of extinction because of hunting. Write a report and remember the stages:
   - research
   - making notes (on the facts you need)
   - ordering your notes (into facts which support hunting and facts which are against hunting)
   - deciding on an introduction and conclusion
   - writing a first draft
   - proofreading/revising
   - present final draft

Life in the factories

In 1750, there were no factories; people worked at home, or in little workshops employing just a few people. One hundred years later, everything had changed, and millions were working in factories. During this period the number of people living in Manchester increased by 20 times, and in Birmingham and Glasgow by nearly as much.

The factories were noisy, dirty, dangerous places, and life was very hard for the factory workers. Men, women and children had to work for up to 18 hours a day, and many accidents occurred because people were so tired. It wasn't until 1847 that Parliament passed a law limiting the working day to 10 hours for women and children.

Children carrying clay in the brickyards of England

Child being paid

Children usually started work at the age of nine, and were harshly punished for not paying attention to their work – even for looking out of the window. It was not just a few unlucky children either. In many factories at this time at least half the workers were children, and at least half of the grown-ups were women; so there would not have been anyone at home to look after the children anyway. There were few schools. Children could go to evening classes, if they were able to stay awake, or to Sunday School, and that was all.

Wages were very low and were often given partly in money and partly in tokens. These tokens could only be spent in the factory shop or "Tommy Shop" where prices were higher and quality was worse than in other shops. This was called the "Truck System", and although the Truck Act was passed in 1831 to forbid it, the practice continued for some years because there was no one to enforce the law.

Those who could not get work had to starve, steal or go to the workhouse. Life in the workhouse was designed to be worse than anywhere else, so that no one would go there if they could possibly help it. Children were separated from their parents, and husbands from their wives. Prison uniforms were worn, the food was very poor, the work was very hard – stone breaking for example – and the inmates could only go out or have visitors with special permission.

The factory worker was not much better off in his own home; it was certain to be dark and airless – there was a tax on windows – and badly built. The big towns and cities grew so quickly that whole families had to live in one room, and many people lived in cellars. There was no proper sanitation, water supply, or rubbish collection, and disease was so bad that in 1841 half the children in Liverpool died before the age of 10.

The people wanted Parliament to change things for the better; but only well-off people were allowed to vote, and the big towns had very few MPs. As a result the Chartist Movement grew up; it held great meetings all over the country, particularly in the North, and organised a huge petition asking for the reform of Parliament. The Chartists also wanted the workhouses to be improved, and asked for the working day to be limited to ten hours. The people also formed trade unions to try to get higher wages and better working conditions, and gradually things began to improve.

From *Tools and Manufacturing* by Gordon Burne

COMPREHENSION

Read the passage and answer the questions.

1 What was the main difference between working life in 1750 and 1850?

2 Make a list of the disadvantages of working life in a factory in the 19th century for:

    a men   b women   c children

3 What happened to those who could not get work?

4 What were the disadvantages of living in a big town or city?

5 In your opinion, was it right that children should start work at the age of nine?

6 For what purpose do you think this passage was written?

WRITING A SUMMARY

Chainmaker

A summary is a shortened version of something that includes all the main points. To write a summary you need to:

● understand what you have read

● write the main points in your own words.

▲ How to make a summary of the passage *Life in the factories*.

Step 1

Look at each paragraph in turn and write down the main points in note form, for example:

Paragraph 1   *1750 – no factories – people worked at home or in small workshops*

     1850 – millions of people worked in factories

     number of people living in towns and cities increased

Paragraph 2   *factories – noisy, dirty, dangerous*

     18 hour work days for men, women and children

     lots of accidents

     1847 – law limiting working day to 10 hours for women and children

▲ Make notes on the main points in paragraphs 3 to 7.

Step 2

Using your own notes, not the original passage, write the first draft of your summary. Use your own words as far as possible. You can use the same number of paragraphs as the original passage but they will be shorter, for example:

Between 1750 and 1850 the working life of many people changed from that of the home or small workshop to factories. The population of towns and cities increased.

    Factories were unpleasant, dirty places where lots of accidents occurred. Men, women and children had to work for 18 hours each day until 1847 when a law was passed so that women and children could only work 10 hours each day.

▲ Use your notes on paragraphs 3 to 7 to finish the first draft of the summary.

Step 3

▲ Proofread and revise your first draft to see that you have:

- included all the main points
- used your own words as far as possible
- used correct spellings, grammar and punctuation
- made your summary *shorter* than the original version.

Step 4

▲ Present your final draft neatly.

OPINIONS – MACHINES: GOOD OR BAD?

The passage *Life in the factories* highlights all the bad things that came with the inventions of machines in the workplace. Many people are of the opinion that machines are a 'necessary evil' whereas some people think that they have greatly improved our lives. One such machine that people have very different views about is the motor car.

Motor Cars

From a city window, 'way up high,
I like to watch the cars go by.
They look like burnished beetles, black,
That leave a little muddy track
Behind them as they slowly crawl.
Sometimes they do not move at all
But huddle close with hum and drone
As though they feared to be alone.
They grope their way through fog and night
With the golden feelers of their light.

Rowena Bennett

COMPREHENSION

Read the poem and answer the questions.

1 In what ways do the cars look like insects?

2 What is the poet's opinion of the motor car?

3 What is your opinion of the motor car?
   Make a list of the advantages and disadvantages.

Cynddylan on a Tractor

Ah, you should see Cynddylan on a tractor.
Gone the old look that yoked him to the soil;
He's a new man now, part of the machine,
His nerves of metal and his blood oil.
The clutch curses, but the gears obey
His least bidding, and lo, he's away
Out of the farmyard, scattering hens.
Riding to work now as a great man should,
He is the knight at arms breaking the fields'
Mirror of silence, emptying the wood
Of foxes and squirrels and bright jays.
The sun comes over the tall trees
Kindling all the hedges, but not for him
Who runs his engine on a different fuel.
And all the birds are singing, bills wide in vain,
As Cynddylan passes proudly up the lane.

R S Thomas

COMPREHENSION

Read the poem and answer the questions.

1 What impression do you get of Cynddylan when the poet says that his nerves are 'metal and his blood oil'?

2 What effect does the tractor have on the animals?

3 What do you think is the purpose of the poem? Think about whether the poet approves or disapproves of the tractor.

WRITING ABOUT OPINIONS

Write about one machine that has changed our lives in a big way. It may be the motor car, the train, the telephone or you may have ideas of your own. Plan your work in the following way:

Stage 1 – **Research**

- Find out when and where your machine was invented and who invented it.

- Ask at least ten people what their opinion of the machine is. You will need to ask them very definite questions such as:

"Do you think life has improved since this machine was invented? Why?"

"Do you think life has become worse since this machine was invented? Why?"

Stage 2 – **Making notes**

Make notes on the answers you get and include your own opinion and reasons.

Stage 3 – **Ordering your notes**

Order your notes by putting all the reasons why life has improved in one list and all the reasons why it has got worse in another.

Stage 4 – **Writing a first draft**

- Begin with a brief introduction about when your machine was invented, by whom and so on.
- Write about the different opinions people have about your machine.
- Write your conclusion.

Stage 5 – **Proofreading and revising**

Stage 6 – **Present the final draft**

PERSONAL CHOICE

Choose one or two of the following assignments:

1   Imagine that you worked in a factory in the nineteenth century before the law was passed limiting a child's working day to ten hours. Write a detailed account of a day at work starting from the time you woke up in the morning and finishing when you went to bed.

2   Invent a machine that will do a boring, everyday task. Design an advertisement for a magazine that will persuade people to buy it.

3   Make a list of all the machines that you use in one day. If those machines did not exist what would you do? Write your alternatives next to each machine.

Moral tales

This is a story from the Buddhist religion which teaches a lesson in a very amusing way. Buddha said:

Friends, long ago in this very city there lived a prince who became weary of listening to the so-called wise men. You see, each of these men of learning had different ideas about the gods and the sacred books, and they used to argue with tongues like razors. One day the prince gathered together in the market place all the blind men in the city. Near them he placed an elephant. Then he told each man to go to the great beast and feel it with his hands. The first blind man advanced to the elephant and felt its head. The second took hold of its ear, the third its tusk, the fourth its trunk, the fifth its foot, the sixth its back, the seventh its tail and the last the tuft of the tail.

"Now then," said the prince, "tell us what an elephant looks like."

The first, who had felt his head, said, "It's like a pot."

The next, the one who had touched the ear, said, "No, an elephant looks like a fan."

"Nonsense!" laughed the man who had fingered the tusk, "it's round, hard and smooth like the handle of a plough."

"Don't be daft," said the one who had felt the trunk. "The elephant is like a snake."

To cut a long story short, each man described the animal differently. So the foot became a pillar, the back a barn, the tail a rope and the tuft a feather-duster. Each of the blind men was sure that he was right and all the others were wrong. At once a furious argument arose. Tempers rose and so did voices. Wild words were flung back and forth. One man punched another. There was a cry of pain. In a few moments the market place was a tangle of fighting bodies.

The city's learned men looked on at all this, amazed and amused. The prince turned to them and said, "I don't know why you're laughing, gentlemen. Your own squabbles are just like these poor fellows'. You have your own narrow view of every question and you can't see anyone else's. You must learn to examine ideas all over, as the blind men should have examined the elephant. You'll never understand anything unless you look at it from many different angles."

From *101 School Assembly Stories* by Frank Carr

COMPREHENSION

Read the story carefully and answer the questions.

1 Why did the prince gather the blind men together?

2 When the blind men were asked to examine the elephant what mistake did they make?

3 What happened when the prince asked them to describe the elephant?

4 Find these words and phrases in the story and explain them in your own words:

a tongues like razors   b to cut a long story short
c wild words   d narrow view of every question

5 What was the prince trying to prove to the wise men?

6 Do you think this was a good way to prove his point?
Give your reasons.

DIFFERENT VERSIONS

Many stories from different religions have survived over hundreds of years but the details are often different from one version to another. Here is another version of the same story.

The Blind Men and the Elephant

It was six men of Hindostan,
  To learning much inclined,
Who went to see the elephant,
  (Though all of them were blind):
That each by observation
  Might satisfy his mind.

The *first* approached the Elephant,
  And happening to fall
Against his broad and sturdy side,
  At once began to bawl:
"Bless me, it seems the Elephant
  Is very like a wall."

The *second*, feeling of his tusk,
  Cried, "Ho! what have we here
So very round and smooth and sharp?
  To me 'tis mighty clear
This wonder of an Elephant
  Is very like a spear."

The *third* approached the animal,
  And happening to take
The squirming trunk within his hands,
  Then boldly up and spake:
"I see," quoth he, "the Elephant
  Is very like a snake."

The *fourth* stretched out his eager hand
    And felt about the knee,
"What most this mighty beast is like
    Is mighty plain," quoth he;
" 'Tis clear enough the Elephant
    Is very like a tree."

The *fifth* who chanced to touch the ear
    Said, "Even the blindest man
Can tell what this resembles most;
    Deny the fact who can,
This marvel of an Elephant
    Is very like a fan."

The *sixth* no sooner had begun
    About the beast to grope,
Than, seizing on the swinging tail
    That fell within his scope,
"I see," cried he, "the Elephant
    Is very like a rope."

And so these men of Hindostan
    Disputed loud and long,
Each in his own opinion
    Exceeding stiff and strong,
Though *each* was *partly* in the right
    And all were in the wrong.

John Godfrey Saxe

1 Read the story and the poem very carefully and make
  notes on:
    a the details that are the same
    b the details that are different.

2 Does the fact that the details in the story differ from those in the
  poem make any difference to the point that is being made?

3 Which of the two do you think makes its point most strongly?
  Explain how it does this.

AESOP'S FABLES

We know very little about the man Aesop except that he probably lived in Greece in the middle of the sixth century. He is known to us as the author of many fables which teach valuable lessons.

▲ Read each fable carefully before writing about what lesson it is trying to teach.

A lion was just going to eat a hare which was sleeping in the grass, when he saw a deer run by. He left the hare to chase after the deer. The hare, hearing all the noise, jumped up. After a long time the lion got tired and could not catch the deer. He went back to get the hare, but he found that it too had run away.

A tortoise wanted an eagle to teach it to fly. The eagle thought that this was a silly idea as the tortoise had no wings. The tortoise only begged him more, so the eagle agreed. He gripped the tortoise in his talons, took him to a great height and let go. The tortoise fell on to some rocks and was broken into pieces.

A crow caught in a trap promised to offer incense to the god Apollo if he would help him. Apollo freed him from the trap and immediately the crow forgot his promise. Some time later the crow was caught again. He promised a sacrifice to another god called Hermes. But Hermes was not willing to help him because of the way he had treated Apollo.

Decide what lesson you want to teach through your fable. Here are a few suggestions, but you might like to think of your own:

> look before you leap
>
> once bitten, twice shy
>
> know your limitations
>
> things are not always what they seem

- Think about **the characters** you need in the fable. Many of Aesop's fables use animals but they can talk and often act like humans. This is called **anthropomorphism**.

- Think about **the plot** – what is going to happen. Fables are usually quite short. Their purpose is to teach a lesson, not to be exciting or frightening etc. like other sorts of stories that you have learnt to write.

- **The setting** is not as important in a fable as in other kinds of stories. What you need to concentrate on is the action of the characters which clearly shows the lesson to be learned.

Choose one or two of the following assignments:

Ask your teacher for a photocopy of the 'playscript planning sheet'.

1 Write a playscript for *The Blind Men and the Elephant*. Remember to include:

    the setting – how many scenes will you need?
    the characters – will you need characters who do not speak, as well as those who do?
    the dialogue – who is going to say what?
    the stage directions – how are the characters going to behave?

2 Write a fable that teaches the lesson 'One good turn deserves another'. Put it into cartoon form or a picture book for a small child.

The mystery of the *Mary Celeste*

On 5th December, 1872, the *Dei Gratia*, a ship sailing from New York to Gibraltar, came across a two-masted square-rigger in the middle of the ocean. Her course was unsteady, going this way and that with the wind. As the *Dei Gratia* got closer the captain could see that no one was at the helm. He signalled to the strange ship but there was no reply.

Lowering a rowing boat into the water, the captain, the second mate and two other sailors made their way over to the ship. As they got closer the name on the stern became visible. It was the *Mary Celeste.*

The captain and the mate climbed aboard, expecting to be greeted by members of the crew, but what they found was a mystery that they could not explain then, and which to this day has remained unsolved.

They made a thorough search of the ship only to find that it was completely deserted. The ship itself was in excellent condition. There was plenty of food and water and the cargo, barrels of alcohol, was intact and in place in the hold.

The Mary Celeste 1872

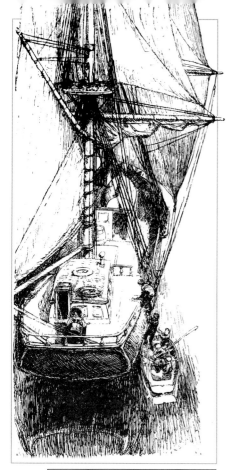

In the captain's cabin they found the table laid for a breakfast which had only been half-eaten and in the galley, pots containing food hung over a dead fire. In the mate's cabin there was a piece of paper on the desk on which was written a half-finished calculation. The only thing that appeared to be missing was the ship's chronometer.

The captain of the *Dei Gratia* suspected there had been a mutiny but as the lifeboat was still there it was impossible to see how the crew had escaped. Had they been taken off by a passing ship? Had they jumped overboard? There were, however, some suspicious clues. In one cabin there was a cutlass smeared with blood and there were similar stains on the deck rail.

The last entry in the log was dated 24th November, ten days before the *Dei Gratia* had come across her. The log indicated that the *Mary Celeste* had been passing north of St Mary's Island in the Azores. If she had been abandoned soon after that then there was no way she would have drifted to this spot. The way her sails were set she could not have reached where she was unless someone had been sailing her.

An official inquiry came up with an explanation that did not hold water. It decided that the most likely course of events was that the crew had murdered the captain and his family and had then escaped on another vessel. However, there was no sign of a struggle and no valuables were taken. Other popular theories abounded. It was suggested that the ship had been attacked by an octopus or some such monster which had taken the crew but left the ship completely undamaged! Had the ship come across a mysterious, unknown island? Had they been sucked off the decks by some bizarre whirlwind? Whatever the fate of the crew of the *Mary Celeste*, it remains a mystery to this day.

COMPREHENSION

Read the passage and answer the questions.

1 Across which ocean was the *Dei Gratia* sailing when she sighted the *Mary Celeste*?

2 Why is the *Mary Celeste* described as 'strange' in the opening paragraph?

3 What did the captain and the mate find that suggested the ship was in perfect order?

4 What did they find that was out of the ordinary?

5 The captain of the *Dei Gratia* and the official inquiry, came to the conclusion that there had been a mutiny. Why was this explanation not very likely?

6 What do **you** think might have happened to the *Mary Celeste*?

When writing a mystery story the main aim is to keep the readers guessing what will happen to the very end. Sometimes, in fact, the mystery is not solved and the readers must use their own imagination to explain the mysterious happenings in the story.

▲ The account of the *Mary Celeste* can be used as a basis for a mystery story. You have the facts of what happened as far as they are known but to make it more exciting you will need to think carefully about other details you can add throughout the story.

A story (fiction) based on fact is sometimes called **faction**.

Setting

- the story will begin aboard the *Dei Gratia*
- the main events will take place on the *Mary Celeste*
- there will be an inquiry by the British Admiralty's Gibraltar office

Characters

- the captain of the *Dei Gratia*
- the second mate
- other members of the crew
- the people holding the inquiry
- any other character(s) you wish to introduce

Plot

- the *Dei Gratia* comes across the *Mary Celeste*
- the captain and second mate go aboard
- they discover that the ship is empty
- they sail to Gibraltar
- the inquiry
- your own ending

▲ Before you begin writing you need to think carefully about:

1 **How you will begin your story.**

Mystery stories often use **contrast**. The opening of your story could be quite ordinary; the *Dei Gratia* is sailing along on a very ordinary day before she encounters the *Mary Celeste*. The mystery begins when the captain and crew realise there is something strange about the ship.

74

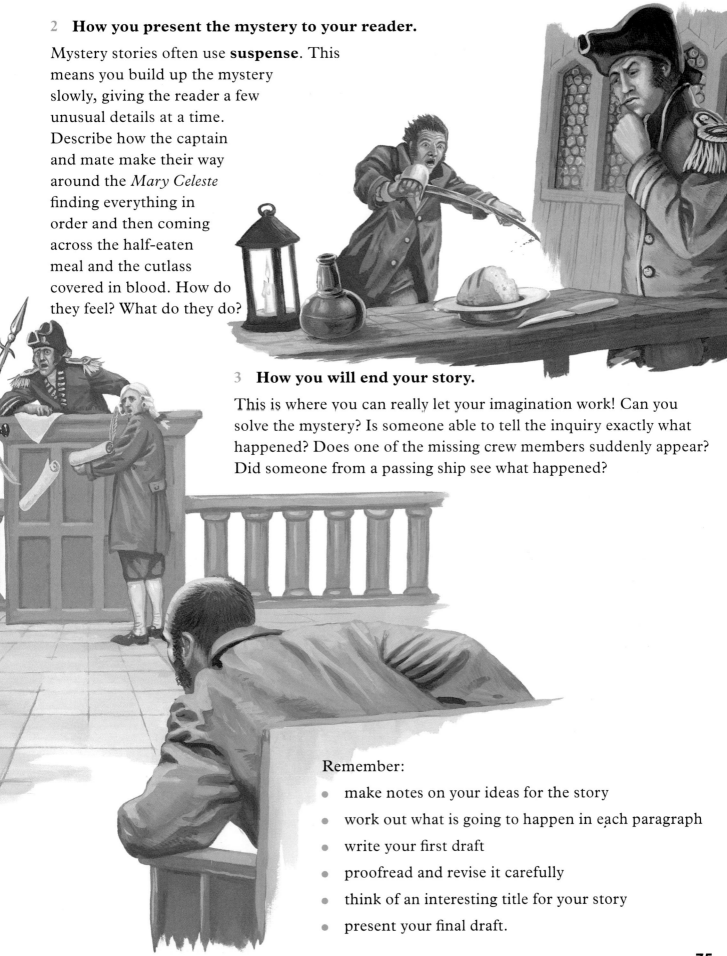

2 How you present the mystery to your reader.

Mystery stories often use **suspense**. This means you build up the mystery slowly, giving the reader a few unusual details at a time. Describe how the captain and mate make their way around the *Mary Celeste* finding everything in order and then coming across the half-eaten meal and the cutlass covered in blood. How do they feel? What do they do?

3 How you will end your story.

This is where you can really let your imagination work! Can you solve the mystery? Is someone able to tell the inquiry exactly what happened? Does one of the missing crew members suddenly appear? Did someone from a passing ship see what happened?

Remember:

- make notes on your ideas for the story
- work out what is going to happen in each paragraph
- write your first draft
- proofread and revise it carefully
- think of an interesting title for your story
- present your final draft.

The Listeners

'Is there anybody there?' said the Traveller,
    Knocking on the moonlit door;
And his horse in the silence champed the grasses
    Of the forest's ferny floor:
And a bird flew up out of the turret,
    Above the Traveller's head:
And he smote upon the door again a second time;
    'Is there anybody there?' he said.
But no one descended to the Traveller;
    No head from the leaf-fringed sill
Leaned over and looked into his grey eyes,
    Where he stood perplexed and still.
But only a host of phantom listeners
    That dwelt in the lone house then
Stood listening in the quiet of the moonlight
    To that voice from the world of men:
Stood thronging the faint moonbeams on the dark stair,
    That goes down to the empty hall,
Hearkening in an air stirred and shaken
    By the lonely Traveller's call.
And he felt in his heart their strangeness,
    Their stillness answering his cry,
While his horse moved, cropping the dark turf,
    'Neath the starred and leafy sky;
For he suddenly smote on the door, even
    Louder, and lifted his head: –
'Tell them I came, and no one answered,
    That I kept my word,' he said.
Never the least stir made the listeners,
    Though every word he spake
Fell echoing through the shadowiness of the still house
    From the one man left awake:
Ay, they heard his foot upon the stirrup,
    And the sound of iron on stone,
And how the silence surged softly backward,
    When the plunging hoofs were gone.

Walter De La Mare

POETRY STUDY

This is a very mysterious poem with lots of questions unanswered:

- who is 'the Traveller'?
- why has he gone to the house?
- who is he expecting to meet there?
- who are the 'phantom listeners'?
- why is there no one there to meet him?
- what is the promise he made?
- why is he described as 'the one man left awake'?

▲ Write two paragraphs about the poem:

paragraph 1   What you think is happening in the poem. Can you solve the mystery?

paragraph 2   How the poem makes you feel. Say whether you like or dislike it and explain why.

PERSONAL CHOICE

Choose one of the following assignments:

1   Design a book cover for a story called 'The Mystery of the *Mary Celeste*'. Include the title and author on the front and write a book blurb on the back cover which will make people want to read the book.

2   Imagine you are the second mate aboard the *Dei Gratia*. You have to write a report of the events of the day you found the *Mary Celeste* that will be read out in court. You must stick to the facts as you know them and be as precise as possible about what you saw and where you found things.

3   Write your own 'mysterious' poem. Imagine you are one of the listeners not answering the door.

Weird and wonderful

The Legend of Alderley

At dawn one still October day in the long ago of the world, across the hill of Alderley, a farmer from Mobberley was riding to Macclesfield fair.

The morning was dull, but mild; light mists bedimmed his way; the woods were hushed; the day promised fine. The farmer was in good spirits, and he let his horse, a milk-white mare, set her own pace, for he wanted her to arrive fresh for the market. A rich man would walk back to Mobberley that night.

So, his mind in the town while he was yet on the hill, the farmer drew near to the place known as Thieves' Hole. And there the horse stood still and would answer to neither spur nor rein. The spur and rein she understood, and her master's stern command, but the eyes that held her were stronger than all these.

In the middle of the path, where surely there had been no one, was an old man, tall, with long hair and beard. "You go to sell this mare," he said. "I come here to buy. What is your price?"

But the farmer wished to sell only at the market, where he would have a choice of many offers, so he rudely bade the stranger quit the path and let him through, for if he stayed longer he would be late to the fair.

"Then go your way," said the old man. "None will buy. And I shall await you here at sunset."

The next moment he was gone, and the farmer could not tell how or where.

The day was warm, and the tavern cool, and all who saw the mare agreed that she was a splendid animal, the pride of Cheshire, a queen among horses; and everyone said that there was no finer beast in the town. But no one offered to buy. A sour-eyed farmer rode out of Macclesfield at the end of the day.

Near Thieves' Hole the mare stopped: the stranger was there.

Thinking any price was now better than none, the farmer agreed to sell. "How much will you give?" he said.

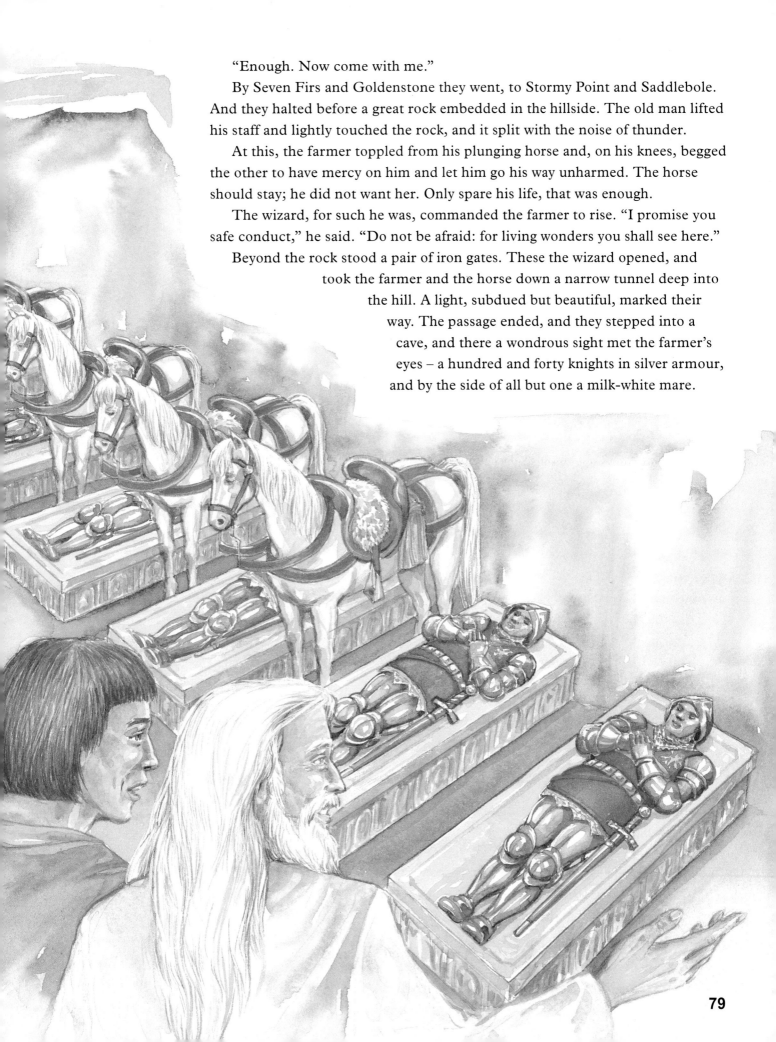

"Enough. Now come with me."

By Seven Firs and Goldenstone they went, to Stormy Point and Saddlebole. And they halted before a great rock embedded in the hillside. The old man lifted his staff and lightly touched the rock, and it split with the noise of thunder.

At this, the farmer toppled from his plunging horse and, on his knees, begged the other to have mercy on him and let him go his way unharmed. The horse should stay; he did not want her. Only spare his life, that was enough.

The wizard, for such he was, commanded the farmer to rise. "I promise you safe conduct," he said. "Do not be afraid: for living wonders you shall see here."

Beyond the rock stood a pair of iron gates. These the wizard opened, and took the farmer and the horse down a narrow tunnel deep into the hill. A light, subdued but beautiful, marked their way. The passage ended, and they stepped into a cave, and there a wondrous sight met the farmer's eyes – a hundred and forty knights in silver armour, and by the side of all but one a milk-white mare.

"Here they lie in enchanted sleep," said the wizard, "until the day will come – and come it will – when England shall be in direst peril, and England's mothers weep. Then out from the hill these must ride and, in a battle thrice lost, thrice won, upon the plain, drive the enemy into the sea."

The farmer, dumb with awe, turned with the wizard into a further cavern, and here mounds of gold and silver and precious stones lay strewn along the ground.

"Take what you can carry in payment for the horse."

And when the farmer had crammed his pockets (ample as his lands!), his shirt, and his fists with jewels, the wizard hurried him up the long tunnel and thrust him out of the gates. The farmer stumbled, the thunder rolled, he looked, and there was only the rock above him. He was alone on the hill, near Stormy Point. The broad full moon was up, and it was night.

And although in later years he tried to find the place, neither he nor any after him ever saw the iron gates again. Nell Beck swore she saw them once, but she was said to be mad, and when she died they buried her under a hollow bank near Brindlow Wood in the field that bears her name to this day.

The Weirdstone of Brisingamen by Alan Garner

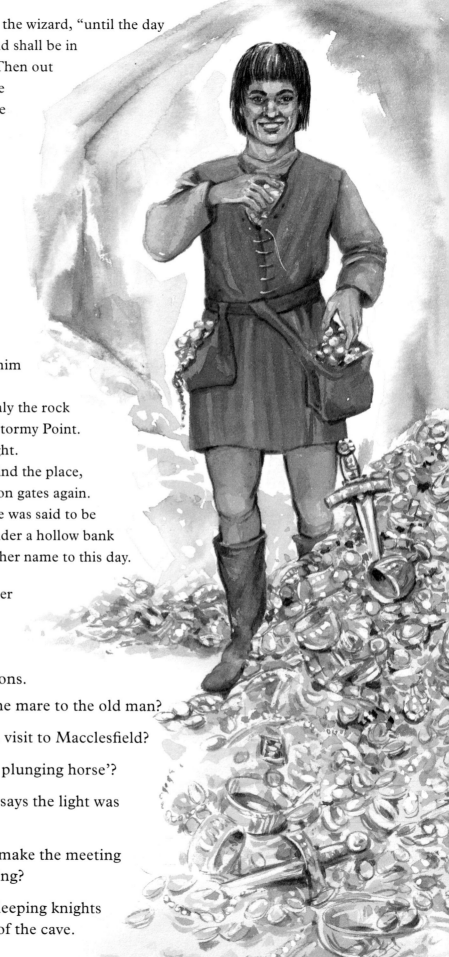

COMPREHENSION

Read the passage and answer the questions.

1   Why didn't the farmer want to sell the mare to the old man?

2   What was strange about the farmer's visit to Macclesfield?

3   Why did the farmer topple from 'his plunging horse'?

4   What does the writer mean when he says the light was 'subdued but beautiful'?

5   How does the writer use contrast to make the meeting with the strange old man more exciting?

6   Write, in your own words, why the sleeping knights would one day awake and come out of the cave.

WRITING A PLAYSCRIPT

Write *The Legend of Alderley* as a playscript. You must include:

The scenes/settings

Work out how many places there are in the story. This is quite easy if you think of the different places that the farmer goes to. Give each scene a number and a short title, for example:

Scene One: Across the hill of Alderley

The characters

There are two main characters in the story. Who are they?
In one of the scenes other characters say things but they are not given names. You will have to choose names for them.

The dialogue

This is what the characters say. You can use the spoken words from the story but you might have to add some of your own.

The stage directions

These tell the characters what they have to do and how they have to speak, for example:

(The farmer is riding along in a good mood.)

(The farmer looks a little frightened.)

Put your stage directions in brackets so it is clear that the characters do not speak these words.

Jabberwocky

'Twas brillig, and the slithy toves
    Did gyre and gimble in the wabe:
All mimsy were the borogoves,
    And the mome raths outgrabe.

"Beware the Jabberwock, my son!
    The jaws that bite, the claws that catch!
Beware the Jubjub bird, and shun
    The frumious Bandersnatch!"

He took his vorpal sword in hand:
    Long time the manxome foe he sought—
So rested he by the Tumtum tree,
    And stood awhile in thought.

And, as in uffish thought he stood,
    The Jabberwock, with eyes of flame,
Came whiffling through the tulgey wood,
    And burbled as it came!

One, two! One, two! And through and through
    The vorpal blade went snicker-snack!
He left it dead, and with its head
    He went galumphing back.

"And hast thou slain the Jabberwock?
    Come to my arms, my beamish boy!
O frabjous day! Callooh! Callay!"
    He chortled in his joy.

'Twas brillig, and the slithy toves
    Did gyre and gimble in the wabe:
All mimsy were the borogoves,
    And the mome raths outgrabe.

Lewis Carroll

When asked to choose a favourite poem, one boy chose *Jabberwocky*. One of his reasons was "because it has so many made-up words. These words are weird words but one can always make out what they mean – words like 'slithy' which I think means 'slimy'."

1 Write, in your own words, what you think is happening in the poem.

2 Make a list of all the 'weird words' in the poem and then try to write what you think each one means.

PERSONAL CHOICE   Choose one or two of the following assignments:

1 In *The Legend of Alderley* one of the sleeping knights does not have a horse. Write a story to explain why he has no horse.

2 Imagine you are the farmer in *The Legend of Alderley* and write a letter to a friend describing what happened to you on the day you met the old man near Thieves' Hole.

3 In the poem *Jabberwocky*, the Jabberwock is killed but there is still the Jubjub bird and the Bandersnatch! Add two more verses to the poem saying what happens when the son meets these two creatures. Remember you can use as many made-up words as you like!

Danger on the cliff!

When writing a story, the author gives clues so that the reader can predict what might happen. Sometimes a reader's prediction can be totally wrong, as the writer puts something unexpected in the story. Sometimes a reader can predict several things that could happen, only some of which might be true.

Read the beginning of the following story – *The Iron Man* by Ted Hughes – stopping each time you are asked a question in red about what happens next. Write what you think might happen and then read on to see if you are right.

Chapter One – The Coming of the Iron Man

The Iron Man came to the top of the cliff.

How far had he walked? Nobody knows. Where had he come from? Nobody knows. How was he made? Nobody knows.

Taller than a house, the Iron Man stood at the top of the cliff, on the very brink, in the darkness.

The wind sang through his iron fingers. His great iron head, shaped like a dustbin but as big as a bedroom, slowly turned to the right, slowly turned to the left. His iron ears turned, this way, that way. He was hearing the sea. His eyes, like headlamps, glowed white, then red, then infra-red, searching the sea. Never before had the Iron Man seen the sea.

He swayed in the strong wind that pressed against his back. He swayed forward, on the brink of the high cliff.

1 **What do you think happens next?**

And his right foot, his enormous iron right foot, lifted – up, out, into space, and the Iron Man stepped forward, off the cliff, into nothingness.

CRRRAAAASSSSSSH!

Down the cliff the Iron Man came toppling, head over heels.

CRASH!

CRASH!

CRASH!

From rock to rock, snag to snag, tumbling slowly. And as he crashed and crashed and crashed

2 What do you think happens to the Iron Man?

His iron legs fell off.

His iron arms broke off, and the hands broke off the arms.

His great iron ears fell off and his eyes fell out.

His great iron head fell off.

All the separate pieces tumbled, scattered, crashing, bumping, clanging, down on to the rocky beach far below.

A few rocks tumbled with him.

Then

Silence.

Only the sound of the sea, chewing away at the edge of the rocky beach, where the bits and pieces of the Iron Man lay scattered far and wide, silent and unmoving.

Only one of the iron hands, lying beside an old, sand-logged washed-up seaman's boot, waved its fingers for a minute, like a crab on its back. Then it lay still.

While the stars went on wheeling through the sky and the wind went on tugging at the grass on the cliff-top and the sea went on boiling and booming.

Nobody knew the Iron Man had fallen.

3 Do you think this is the end of the Iron Man?

Night passed.

Just before dawn, as the darkness grew blue and the shapes of the rocks separated from each other, two seagulls flew crying over the rocks. They landed on a patch of sand. They had two chicks in a nest on the cliff. Now they were searching for food.

One of the seagulls flew up – Aaaaaark! He had seen something. He glided low over the sharp rocks. He landed and picked something up. Something shiny, round and hard.

4   What do you think the seagull had found?

It was one of the Iron Man's eyes. He brought it back to his mate. They both looked at this strange thing. And the eye looked at them. It rolled from side to side looking first at one gull, then at the other. The gulls, peering at it, thought it was a strange kind of clam, peeping at them from its shell.

Then the other gull flew up, wheeled around and landed and picked something up. Some awkward, heavy thing. The gull flew low and slowly, dragging the heavy thing. Finally, the gull dropped it beside the eye. This new thing had five legs. It moved. The gulls thought it was a strange kind of crab. They thought they had found a strange crab and a strange clam.

5   What do you think the other gull has found?

They did not know they had found the Iron Man's eye and the Iron Man's right hand.

But as soon as the eye and the hand got together the eye looked at the hand. Its light glowed blue. The hand stood up on three fingers and its thumb, and craned its forefinger like a long nose. It felt around. It touched the eye. Gleefully it picked up the eye, and tucked it under its middle finger. The eye peered out, between the forefinger and thumb. Now the hand could see.

6   What do you think the eye and the hand do now?

86

LOOKING FOR CLUES

Were you right in your predictions?
Ted Hughes gives the reader some clues. Did you spot them?

1   At this point in the story you could have predicted that the Iron
    Man was going to fall off the cliff.
    What clues in the story so far would lead you to predict this?

2   Here the Iron Man is very badly damaged.
    *What clues does Ted Hughes give you so you can predict that
    this might happen?*

3   This is not so easy to predict.
    *Did you look at the title of the story and the number and title
    of the chapter?*

4   The gull had found the Iron Man's eye.
    What clues would help you predict this?

5   The other gull had found the Iron Man's hand.
    What clues would help you predict this?

6   The hand and the eye go looking for the rest of the Iron Man.
    What clues would help you predict this?

USING THE CLUES

1   Read the beginning of *The Iron Man* again and make notes
    on the following:

- the setting
- the characters: the Iron Man and the gulls
- the plot so far.

2   Using these notes write an ending for the first chapter, from
    when the hand and eye are together to when they have found
    the rest of the Iron Man and he is in one piece again.

BOOK REVIEWS

The purpose of a book review is to help other people decide if they would like to read a particular book. It should include:

- the author and title

- the type of book – fiction, non-fiction, poetry, etc.

- the age of the audience the book is written for – very young children, juniors, teenagers, etc.

- a brief summary of the story – without giving away the ending

- the personal opinion of the reviewer – interesting, exciting, frightening, etc.

▲ Read the book review of *The Iron Man* and answer the questions:

The Iron Man by Ted Hughes is a modern fairy story that can be enjoyed by children and adults alike. The main character, the Iron Man, is seen at the beginning of the story falling down a cliff and smashing to pieces. Hughes imaginatively tells how the Iron Man reconstructs himself and continues his travels, frightening all who see him. The various attempts to destroy him turn into pleas for help when the space-bat-angel-dragon arrives. Will the Iron Man be able to save the world? The book is beautifully written and keeps you turning the pages until the very end.

1 What is the book called?

2 Who is the author?

3 What type of book is it?

4 Which audience is the book written for?

5 Write a brief summary of the plot in your own words.

6 What does the reviewer think of the book?

WRITING YOUR OWN BOOK REVIEW

1 Choose a book you have read and enjoyed recently.

2 If the book is fiction then follow the list of things on the opposite page that you should include.

3 If the book is non-fiction then the list is the same except for the plot. Instead of writing a summary of the plot you will:

- give the reader an idea of what sort of information is in the book
- say how that information is presented – maps, charts, diagrams, pictures, etc.
- say how clearly the text is written
- say whether, in your opinion, the material is effectively and attractively presented
- say how useful you found it.

4 Now write your book review.

PERSONAL CHOICE

A book blurb tells the reader enough to make them want to read the book, but not enough to spoil the story.

Choose one of the following assignments:

1 Design a book cover for *The Iron Man* and write a book blurb to go with it. Think carefully about the differences between a blurb and a review.

2 Imagine that you meet the Iron Man and you are not afraid of him. You want to know the answers to the questions at the beginning of the story:

How far had he walked?
Where had he come from?
How was he made?

Write the conversation you have with the Iron Man in which he answers all of your questions.

Cats

The Cat Family

wildcat – Found in Europe and West Africa. Approximately 75 cm long with a bushy rounded tail and thick, striped coat. Lives in dense woodlands.

jaguar – Found in southern USA, central and South America. 2.5 m long with a yellow coat marked with dark rosette-shaped spots. It lives in forests and scrub and can swim very well. It hunts peccaries, turtles, capybaras and will attack livestock.

leopard – Found in Africa and Asia. Yellow coat spotted with black rosettes. There are colour variations such as the panther. It preys on monkeys, dogs and antelopes.

puma – Also known as the cougar, mountain lion or catamount. Found in North and South America. It is red/brown in colour, 1.5 to 3 m long, slender and muscular. Main food is deer but will eat a variety of other animals.

snow leopard – Also known as an ounce. It inhabits the mountains of central Asia. 1.9 m long with a thick ash-grey coat marked with dark rosettes. It hunts mountain goats, sheep and marmots.

tiger – Found in central and south Asia. Reddish-fawn coat with black stripes. Hunts at night, mainly antelope.

cheetah – Found in Africa and south west Asia and is also known as the hunting leopard. 2 m long with a reddish-yellow coat with black spots. It is the fastest mammal, reaching speeds of up to 110 kph.

domestic cat – There are a large variety of breeds, thought to have developed from the African and European wildcat.

lion – Found mainly in Africa. 2.8 m long with a sandy-coloured coat. Lives in grasslands.

COMPREHENSION

Read the information about the 'cat' family and answer the questions.

1 What is the snow leopard also called?

2 Where does the wildcat live?

3 Which is the fastest mammal?

4 Which of the cats can swim very well?

5 When does the tiger hunt?

6 What is the puma also known as?

7 What is the lion's habitat?

Cat-Poem

I let you walk all over me,
wet feet and all, before you lie
uncomfortably across my lap.

Soon you are stretched belly upward,
mouth a useful leather purse,
paws limp with mice you've let go.

Or you cling like a cravat
to my chest, and I patch
my days with your black shape.

I try to figure you out, prise
you with words, but you are not
domesticable, and remain beyond call.

Joan Downar

The Cheshire Cat

Alice has just had an extraordinary time with the Duchess and things do not get any less unusual when she meets the Cheshire Cat!

The Cat only grinned when it saw Alice. It looked good-natured, she thought: still it had *very* long claws and a great many teeth, so she felt that it ought to be treated with respect.

"Cheshire Puss," she began, rather timidly, as she did not at all know whether it would like the name: however, it only grinned a little wider. "Come, it's pleased so far," thought Alice, and she went on. "Would you tell me, please, which way I ought to go from here?"

"That depends a good deal on where you want to get to," said the Cat.

"I don't much care where—" said Alice.

"Then it doesn't matter which way you go," said the Cat.

"—so long as I get *somewhere*," Alice added as an explanation.

"Oh, you're sure to do that," said the Cat, "if you only walk long enough."

Alice felt that this could not be denied, so she tried another question. "What sort of people live about here?"

"In *that* direction," the Cat said, waving its right paw round, "lives a Hatter: and in *that* direction," waving the other paw, "lives a March Hare. Visit either you like: they're both mad."

"But I don't want to go among mad people," Alice remarked.

"Oh, you can't help that," said the Cat: "we're all mad here. I'm mad. You're mad."

"How do you know I'm mad?" said Alice.

"You must be," said the Cat, "or you wouldn't have come here."

Alice didn't think that proved it at all: however, she went on: "And how do you know that you're mad?"

"To begin with," said the Cat, "a dog's not mad. You grant that?"

"I suppose so," said Alice.

"Well, then," the Cat went on, "you see a dog growls when it's angry, and wags its tail when it's pleased. Now *I* growl when I'm pleased, and wag my tail when I'm angry. Therefore I'm mad."

"*I* call it purring, not growling," said Alice.

"Call it what you like," said the Cat. "Do you play croquet with the Queen to-day?"

"I should like it very much," said Alice, "but I haven't been invited yet."

"You'll see me there," said the Cat, and vanished.

From *Alice in Wonderland* by Lewis Carroll

COMPREHENSION

The three pieces of writing – *The Cat Family*, *Cat-Poem* and *The Cheshire Cat* – all share the theme of cats. Each, however, is writing about very different aspects of the theme in a very different way. Look at each piece in turn and answer the following questions:

1 What type of writing is it?

2 For what purpose do you think it was written?

3 For what audience do you think it was written?

4 Does it rely on facts or the imagination?

5 In what kind of book would you find it?

Write about cats in four very different ways or styles. The way
you write will be different because each piece of writing has a
different purpose and will be written for a different audience.

1 Choose **one** piece of writing from **each** of the two cats below.
   Choose **one** piece of writing from **each** of the two cats on page 96.
   You will do **four** pieces of writing in all.

NARRATIVE

ghost story
adventure story
science-fiction story **or**
picture story with text

DESCRIPTIVE

describe the cat
asleep **or** at play
in prose **or**
in poetry

Remember:
- plot
- characters
- setting
- dialogue
- opening/ending
- the first draft
- proofread/revise
- present final draft

Remember:
- adjectives
- adverbs
- details
- the first draft
- proofread/revise
- present final draft

95

FACTUAL
report
diagram
fact file
magazine article **or**
newspaper article

PERSONAL
diary
letter
your own cat **or**
opinion

Remember:

- research
- making notes
- ordering notes
- writing a first draft
- proofread/revise
- present final draft

Remember:

- thoughts and feelings
- writing a first draft
- proofread/revise
- present final draft

2 Decide:

a whether you are going to write about one type of cat or cats in general.

b whether your writing is going to be presented to the rest of the class as:

	illustrations
a wall display	headings
	layout
OR	
	title
a small book	illustrations
	layout
	blurb